The
INDEPENDENCE SQUARE
NEIGHBORHOOD

Ben Collins

The INDEPENDENCE SQUARE *Neighborhood*

Historical Notes on Independence *and* Washington Squares, *Lower* Chestnut Street, *and the* Insurance District *along* Walnut Street, *in* Philadelphia, *together with some Account of the* Buildings, Events, *and* Personages *of* State House Row

---

Illustrated with Photographs, Sketches, *and* Old Prints

PHILADELPHIA   MCMXXVII

Published by The Penn Mutual Life Insurance Company, *from the Home Office* on Independence Square

This story of the Independence Square Neighborhood was written by Carroll Frey. Most of the sketches are from the Old Philadelphia Collection by Frank H. Taylor, and the majority of the photographs are by Philip B. Wallace, who specializes on State House Row. Among the numerous authorities consulted, we especially mention the "History of Philadelphia," by J. Thomas Scharf and Thompson Westcott; "Independence Hall," by Frank M. Etting; the "Independence Hall Bulletins" published by the Philadelphia Department of Public Works; and "Byways and Boulevards In and About Historic Philadelphia," by Francis Burke Brandt and Henry Volkmar Gummere. Acknowledgment also is gratefully made of help from officials of the Historical Society of Pennsylvania, and from William S. Ashbrook and Linden T. Harris of the Neighborhood. The book is engraved and printed by The Beck Engraving Company, in Philadelphia.

SECOND EDITION

COPYRIGHT 1926
THE PENN MUTUAL LIFE
INSURANCE COMPANY

CONTENTS

PAGE

I. THE NEIGHBORHOOD

Independence Square 3
Philadelphia in 1776 11
The Capital City 15
The Neighborhood To-day 25
The Influence of Franklin 29
Lower Chestnut Street 39
Around Independence Square 47
Washington Square 51
The Insurance District 63
The Old Churches 73
Romantic Houses 79

II. STATE HOUSE ROW

Independence Hall 91
Congress Hall 103
Supreme Court Building 105
The First Continental Congress 111
The Declaration of Independence 119
The Articles of Confederation 131
The Federal Constitution 135
The Liberty Bell 145

Independence Hall from the Square.

THE NEIGHBORHOOD

Independence Square

WHEN the provincial authorities of Pennsylvania had builded their State House on Chestnut Street in Philadelphia, and had planned to add a City Building and a County Building on the same plot of ground, with the thought that the finest public edifice in the British Colonies should have a dignified setting they acquired enough additional ground to extend the State House Yard to Walnut Street, thus providing a full city square. This Yard, as they wrote into the deed of 1769, was "to remain a publick greene and walke forever;" and Independence Square,—together with its corner-to-corner neighbor, Washington Square, which had been set aside by William Penn,—stands to this day in the full spirit of the ideal of the founder of the city for a "greene country towne."

Independence Square to-day is still meadowed with pleasant lawn shaded by tall trees; it still has broad flag-stoned walks and iron hitching posts; and it is still terraced by a low brick wall and fronted by the lovely State House Row. But it is more than a mere

Independence Square and State House Row, from Walnut Street—Sixth Street on the left.

park. The buildings in "the Row,"—Independence Hall, Congress Hall, and the Supreme Court Building—with their historical significance, are the nation's heirlooms, and with the Square constitute a permanent memorial to the fathers of the country and to the great deeds which they wrought.

Because it is the birthplace of American Independence and the home of the Liberty Bell, most venerated of all our patriotic relics, Independence Hall is made a place of pilgrimage by some 900,000 persons every year. They come from every part of the country, from every part of the world, and from every class and condition. Perhaps every American of note has made the pilgrimage; certainly every President of the United States has come, and for many years famous visitors from foreign lands have included this shrine in their visits. This was especially noticeable immediately after the World War, when the leading figures among the Allies came to pay their respects to America, and a not uncommon sight in the neighborhood is that of the First City Troop, in the traditional uniform of Revolutionary days, escorting some distinguished visitor to Independence Hall.

From the earliest days, the Square has been the rendezvous for patriotic gatherings, beginning with those which, with similar mass meetings in other Colonial towns, precipitated the armed resistance to the King's troops, and continuing through the excitement and the recruiting at the outbreak of every subsequent war. At great anniversaries and notable elections the interest of Philadelphians centers in Independence Square; there the municipal Christmas tree is placed and

The Continental Congress Voting Independence, 1776. From the painting by Pine and Savage, made about 1783, and which is regarded as much more accurate than the familiar Trumbull painting.

carols sung by a large chorus on Christmas Eve, and there the Independence Hall bell begins the ringing in of the New Year.

State House Row, in the course of its history, has been the seat of government of the city, of the county, of the province, of the state, of the confederation of the colonies and of the nation. "It will forever echo with the voices and footsteps of great men."

In the East Room of the State House, now known as the Declaration Chamber of Independence Hall, George Washington accepted his appointment as General and Commander-in-Chief of the Continental Army, June 16, 1775; the Continental Congress adopted the Declaration of Independence, July 4, 1776, signing it August 2 and thereafter; the Congress adopted the American flag, June 14, 1777; the Articles of Confederation and Perpetual Union between the States were drawn up and signed by the first eight States, July 9, 1778; Congress officially received the news of the surrender of Cornwallis and was presented, November 3, 1781, with twenty-four stands of colors captured at Yorktown; the Federal Convention, between May and September of 1787, framed the Constitution of the United States.

Congress Hall, originally the County Building, was the capitol of the new United States from the beginning of the third session of Congress, 1790, until the seat of national government was removed to Washington, in 1800. In this building Washington was inaugurated for his second term as President of the United States; here he delivered his Farewell Address; and here John Adams was inaugurated President. The first Supreme Court of

The hallway of Independence Hall, through the arch to the tower stairway and the Liberty Bell.

the United States held its sessions in the City Building when the legislative branches met in Congress Hall.

To Independence Square come many visitors who, having made their patriotic pilgrimage, linger to study the architecture of State House Row, which, experts say, "forms a symmetrical group admirably illustrative of the changing phases of our Colonial styles, and a splendid example of the love of formal balance, suggestive also of the tendency to develop and rearrange a preliminary scheme in the course of construction, and the ingenuity and artistic taste of the period which could make a harmonious unit of composite work." The Row was designed in the Georgian English period of architecture, usually called Colonial. The designing of Congress Hall and the Supreme Court Building "shows the delicacy usually considered characteristic of later early American design, which possesses more grace but loses the vigor and monumental character of the Georgian English period which marks the State House."

The interior of Independence Hall is impressive and dignified, with its arches, pilasters, and wainscoting, all in white, and its great stairway lighted by the Palladian window. To one standing in the Declaration Chamber, it should not be difficult to reconstruct in imagination the scene on July 4, 1776, when the Declaration of Independence was adopted; or the scene on August 2, when the engrossed Declaration was signed, with Benjamin Franklin remarking that "We must all hang together or most assuredly we shall all hang separately," and John Hancock making his huge clear

*The Palladian window and the southern doorway, the entrance from the
Square into Independence Hall.*

signature which "King George can read without spectacles;" or the scene in the same room nine years later when, independence having been won, the convention met to frame a national Constitution.

Perhaps the wisest thing the caretakers have done is in cherishing the building itself, with its setting, as, in fact, a monument. They have accordingly restored the entire structure so that it now appears, both internally and externally, substantially as it was at the time of the meeting of the Continental Congress. Several of the original pieces of furniture are there, including the president's table and chair; on the table is the silver inkstand used at the signing, and a framed facsimile of the Declaration hangs on the wall; but it is the building itself, and not the few relics it contains, that will, so long as it stands, continue to make its silent appeal to the heart and emotions of every patriot.

Philadelphia in 1776

SUPPOSE a visitor to Philadelphia in the epic year of 1776 to have climbed into the tower of the State House in which he was attending, as a delegate, the sessions of the Continental Congress; in his hands a map of the city, showing a great checkerboard of squares, laid out by William Penn, formed by streets, regularly spaced, running north and south, east and west, between South Street and Vine Street, and between the Delaware and Schuylkill Rivers. The visitor, from his State House tower viewpoint, found the map more a plan than a record, for he could readily see the whole town, of 24,000

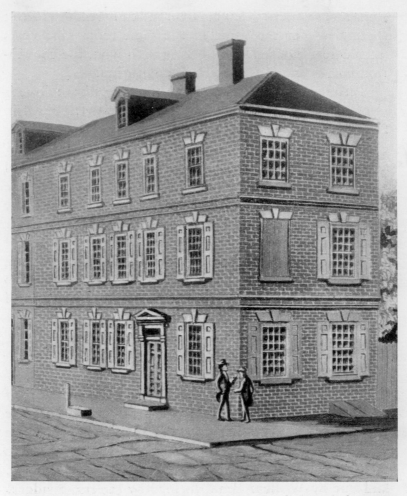

The house at Seventh and Market Streets, on the site of the present Penn National Bank, wherein Thomas Jefferson wrote the Declaration of Independence. From an old print.

population, nestling along the shore of the Delaware River. This birdseye view showed an actual Philadelphia formed like a triangle, with the base covering the city's limits along the river-front, but the one western point, the apex, at about Seventh and Market Streets. Thus the State House was along the West-by-South boundary, and both Southeast (Washington) Square and Northeast (Franklin) Square were just outside of the triangle. West of the triangle were occasional homes and farms and forest. The town of Philadelphia was almost a century old, but it had yet to occupy the first third of the city ground as laid out by Penn's commissioners.

But our visitor, from his tower height, saw "the red city" of Philadelphia, a fine Colonial city almost entirely built of bricks. The principal building was the State House itself, and the several other buildings that caught his eye were: The Carpenters' Hall, a block to the east; the Market, in the middle of Market Street near the river; the Great Meeting House at Second and Market. Several churches: Christ Church, St. Peter's, St. Paul's, St. Joseph's, St. Mary's, St. George's, the First Presbyterian, the Pine Street Presbyterian, the Zion Lutheran, the Methodist; and, of course, the several taverns, one of which was right below, on Chestnut Street opposite the State House. On the other side of the State House Yard, at Sixth and Walnut Streets, was the imposing new prison, only just opened, and two blocks southwest of the Southeast Square, which was the potters' field, was the Pennsylvania Hospital, well out in the woods.

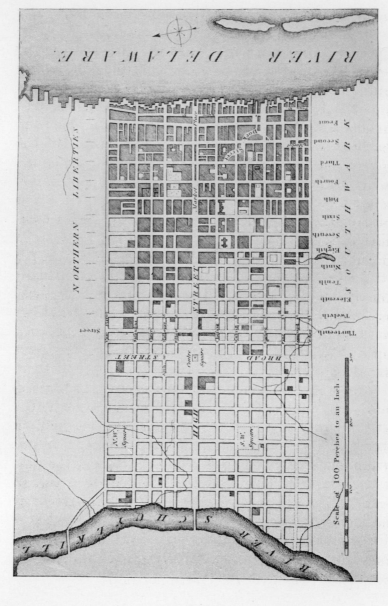

A map of the City of Philadelphia of 1800, of which the limits were Vine and South Streets, and the two rivers. The shaded portions indicate the built-up section. At this time the population had about doubled since 1776.

The Capital City

BUT about twenty years later a visitor to the State House would be in a neighborhood wherein national history had been made. Philadelphia, grown somewhat larger, and with its population doubled, had become the capital of a nation. The State House was soon to be abandoned as the State capitol. And the building, with its wings, had been given two new neighbors, so that the group was known as State House Row; the new County Building, which had been erected at the Sixth Street corner, was occupied by the Congress of the United States; and the new City Building, at the Fifth Street corner, housed the Supreme Court of the United States.

Just back of the City Building was the home of the American Philosophical Society; its similarity of appearance, and the fact that it was the only private building in the State House Yard, might have led many to suppose (as it does to this day) that it was an annex to State House Row.

At the northeast corner of Fifth and Sansom Streets stood the building of the Library Company of Philadelphia, which had been established by Franklin in 1731, and after having been temporarily housed in one of the wings of the State House, and later in the Carpenters' Hall, had finally built here, where it was to remain for almost a century before moving again. At the southeast corner of Fifth and Chestnut Streets was a house wherein Gilbert Stuart, the artist, had his studio, and it was there that President Washington sat for at least two of the celebrated portraits.

Clark's Inn, sometimes called The Coach and Horses because of its sign, and The State House Inn because of its location opposite the State House, on Chestnut Street. From a Smith Ale print.

A few doors below, on Fifth Street, was the building of the first medical school in the city; instituted in 1765, it was usually known as the Surgeon's Hall, and eventually became incorporated with the University of Pennsylvania.

Directly across Chestnut Street from the State House was still the tavern long called the State House Inn, but by now known as the Half Moon, frequented by the provincial and national statesmen. It had been built in 1693, well out of town and across from the meadow which eventually became Independence Square. It stood in a grove of great walnut trees, and because of its rural setting had been something of a favorite spot for William Penn. At one time the tavern was the center of an odd business—the innkeeper trained small dogs to run in cylinders in such a way as to turn the spit for roasting meats at the fireplace.

Just a block to the north, on the southeast corner of Sixth and High (that is, Market) Streets, stood the home of Robert Morris, formerly the executive mansion for the President of the Supreme Council of the State, a position at one time held by John Dickinson, author of "The Farmer's Letters," which had had so much influence in the early days of the Revolution.

Next to the Morris Mansion was a large house which had once been owned by the wife of Governor Richard Penn, had been the headquarters for Lord Howe during the British occupation, and later had been the home of General Benedict Arnold. It had been burned down in 1780; Robert Morris had rebuilt it, and when Philadelphia became the seat of the new national government,

The Executive Mansion on High Street, used by Presidents Washington and Adams. The building to the right, at the Sixth Street corner, was the house of Robert Morris.

President Washington took it over as his executive mansion, and President Adams after him. In the stables to the rear were kept the six white horses and the white coach with which the first President drove about the city.

At Seventh Street, on the southwest corner of Market, was the boarding house ("on the outskirts of the town," as he described it) in which Thomas Jefferson had written the Declaration of Independence. On Seventh Street just above Market was the first United States Mint, which had been built in 1792; David Rittenhouse was the first director, and it is said that the first coins were minted from melted-down silver from the dining room of President Washington.

Just a little north of the northeast corner of Chestnut Street and Sixth was the home and office of Peter Duponceau, a brick dwelling house which was the new nation's Office of Foreign Affairs, first used by Secretary Robert R. Livingston, of New York, who had been on the committee of the Continental Congress which drew up the Declaration, but had been prevented by public business from returning to Philadelphia to sign the engrossed document. As the Office of Foreign Affairs, this humble building was the rendezvous of such international statesmen as Hamilton, Madison, Lafayette, and Rochambeau.

On the southwest corner of Sixth and Chestnut, for a few years of the capital city decade, was Rickett's Circus, a riding school and pantomime, something like a modern hippodrome, and a great favorite with the statesmen.

Where the corners of the State House Yard and

The Walnut Street Prison and the gate in the Walnut Street wall of the State House Yard. From an engraving by Malcom, about 1800.

Southeast Square met, at the southeast corner of Sixth
and Walnut Streets, still stood the Walnut Street Prison,
a great stone, two-story, two-winged building extending
back to Prune (Locust) Street, with smaller outbuildings,
and a high wall around. The first hundred prisoners
had been transferred to the new jail in January of 1776;
they included felons, debtors, prisoners of war, and
Tories, and six of them had celebrated the first night
behind new bars by escaping. When the British had
occupied Philadelphia, during the winter of '77-8, they
had used it as the British Provost Prison, which period
of its career may be found vividly described in S. Weir
Mitchell's novel of the Revolution, "Hugh Wynne."

After the War, and on up until 1836, when it was
torn down, the Walnut Street Prison was to win notoriety
for numerous prison riots and jail deliveries; but its
greatest interest to a later age is perhaps in its record
as a debtors' prison, in which association its most
celebrated inmate, from 1798 to 1801, was the patriot
Robert Morris, signer of the Declaration of Independence,
of the Articles of Confederation, and of the Federal
Constitution, and "Financier of the Revolution."
Incidentally, the most distinguished visitor to the prison
was President Washington, who called and took dinner
with Morris. In his later years Morris lost his great
fortune through business reverses, and within a decade
after his incarceration in this debtors' prison, died,
"poor in purse but rich in honor." It will be recalled
that the founder of Pennsylvania, himself, in his old
age spent nine months as a debtor in Fleet Prison,
London.

The Duponceau House on Sixth Street near Chestnut, about 1796, the first Office of Foreign Affairs of the United States.

To the west, the Walnut Street Prison looked out upon the Southeast Square, which for a century had been the city's potters' field. There is a story that one of the first to be buried therein was a young woman who had taken her own life and who had for that reason been refused a grave in any churchyard, whereupon her whole family had insisted upon accepting this potters' field as their own burial place. Their loyalty must have been prophetic of the unique democracy which had come to rule in this graveyard. Side by side with the paupers and the strangers were buried soldiers of the Revolution, both American and British; criminals from the Prison; and many of the exiled Acadians from Nova Scotia, whose story Longfellow told in his poem, "Evangeline."

In 1777 John Adams wrote in a letter: "I took a walk into the potters' field, and I never in my whole life was so affected with melancholy. The graves of the soldiers who have been buried in the ground from the Hospital and bettering-house during the course of last summer, fall and winter, dead of the smallpox and camp diseases, are enough to make the heart of a stone to melt away. The sexton told me that upwards of two thousand soldiers had been buried there; and by the appearance of the grass and trenches, it is most probable to me that he speaks within bounds. Disease has destroyed ten men for us where the sword of the enemy has killed one."

When the British army had occupied the city, many of its soldiers had died and were interred in the trenches of the potters' field. And the yellow fever epidemic

The first United States Mint was on Seventh Street above Market, on the site of the building of the Stewart Electric Company. It was the first building authorized by the government.

of 1793 had produced so many burials there of citizens of the town that there was little more room, and use of the Square as a potters' field had been gradually abandoned.

The Neighborhood To-day

IN THE days when Independence Hall was the State House, visitors could go up into its high tower and secure a view of all Philadelphia, but to-day the Square is surrounded by taller buildings, largely cutting off the view, so that it would be necessary to go to the roof of one of these higher places. Although one can no longer see more than the mere center of the city, a very interesting view may be had from the roof of, say, the Penn Mutual Building, at Sixth and Walnut.

Independence Square is just below you, to the north, with State House Row along Chestnut Street just a block away, and past the Row the city stretches in an irregular mass of roofs until it disappears in a hazy horizon.

Westward, Washington Square is just below, while some eight blocks away, along Broad Street, clusters the main skyscraper district of the city, where the majority of the taller office buildings and hotels rise above the buildings of average height, which are more characteristic of Philadelphia, a city inclined to spread out rather than to concentrate in real estate. From the northwest, the skyscraper district turns down Market and Chestnut Streets, swinging on down past Independence Square into the financial district along lower Chestnut Street. Directly in front of you is the

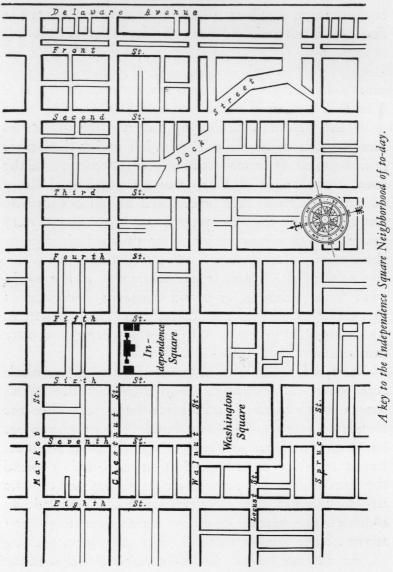

Delaware River

Delaware Avenue

Front St.

Second St.

Dock Street

Third St.

Fourth St.

Fifth St.

In-
dependence Square

Sixth St.

Market St.

Chestnut St.

Walnut St.

Spruce St.

Washington Square

Seventh St.

Locust St.

Eighth St.

A key to the Independence Square Neighborhood of to-day.

Curtis Building, wedging Independence and Washington Squares apart, and just beyond it is the great Benjamin Franklin Hotel, and furthest back and against the sky is City Hall, with its gigantic statue of William Penn atop, at the greatest height in Philadelphia,— a lightning rod protecting the buildings within a radius of a quarter of a mile, it is said.

Toward the south, the three and four story buildings predominate, so that what you see from your high position is mostly rows of roofs, with the long, straight streets cut through right to where the Delaware River swings westerly. And there you can pick out the Navy Yard by the enormous crane, the largest bulk against the southern horizon. Toward the southwest, about three squares away across Washington Square, you can see the Pennsylvania Hospital. Not very far away to the southeast rises the cylindrical building of the Old Shot Tower, which in 1810 was put up in Southwark "to save $200,000 a year sent abroad to buy shot to shoot birds alone."

Eastward, along Walnut Street, starting on Independence Square, is the insurance district of Philadelphia, stretching down to crooked Dock Street, and then the riverfront and the Delaware, and, beyond the river, Camden. Southeasterly on the river, if the day be clear, you may see the great shipbuilding drydocks. Toward the northeast the new Delaware River Bridge, the largest suspension bridge in the world, captures the eye; although ten blocks away, it seems as though you might almost step onto it.

The average visitor would probably be inspired by

The entrance to the Curtis Building on Independence Square—a rainy night.

the view along the River, and by the view toward Broad Street, and he could not fail to be moved by the sylvan beauty of Independence and Washington Squares; but he would doubtless think the view toward the south and west, showing mostly the roofs of buildings of medium and low heights, rather uninteresting. And it is indeed without much interest to anyone who has never seen anything of this district save from a height. But to anyone who will walk through the region with a knowledge of the historical values, the Independence Square neighborhood is packed with interest from a thousand angles.

We are going to walk around Independence Square, stroll down into the financial district of Chestnut Street, return to the Square and around its older sister Square, Washington; and then walk through the famous insurance district which begins at Washington Square. And finally returning to Independence Square, we shall pay a more leisurely visit to State House Row.

The Influence of Franklin

IT IS doubtful if there ever lived a man who was useful to his city in so many varied ways as was Benjamin Franklin to Philadelphia, and the Independence Square neighborhood has reminders of Poor Richard at almost every step. The very streets are policed and paved and cleaned and lighted by municipal departments instituted by Franklin; the graceful, quaint lamps of Independence Square were designed by him. The State House is rich in memories of him, for he was its first

The giants on Independence Square, the Curtis Publishing Company and the Public Ledger Buildings. Looking across the Square from the southeast.

Clerk of the Assembly; he was once President of the Supreme Executive Council of Pennsylvania, and he was a member of the Continental Congress and of the Constitutional Convention which met therein, and he was a signer of the Declaration. In Congress Hall, he was a member of Congress.

If, standing on the pavement of Independence Hall, you will look at the roofs of the buildings on the opposite side of Chestnut Street, you will see a water tank marked: "The Franklin Printing Company, Founded 1728 by Benjamin Franklin." The printing house is located perhaps fifty yards from where you stand,—at 518 Ludlow Street. The business was originally "on High Street, near the Market." Thus, although even in his lifetime it passed out of his hands, Franklin's printing business still continues.

To your left are two huge modern brick buildings continuing his publishing ventures. Both face east on Independence Square. At Walnut and Sixth and Sansom is the Curtis Publishing Company, with its Saturday Evening Post, founded 1821 on Franklin's Pennsylvania Gazette, which had been instituted in 1728; the Post was bought by Cyrus H. K. Curtis in 1898, and now has the largest circulation of any magazine published.

At Chestnut and Sixth and Sansom stands the building of the Public Ledger, founded 1836 by Swain, Abell and Simmons, made famous by George W. Childs, and acquired by Curtis in 1912; in 1925 the Ledger absorbed the North American, the oldest daily newspaper in the country by virtue of its development from Franklin's Pennsylvania Gazette.

The Building of the American Philosophical Society, in Independence Square. A view from the East Arcade of State House Row.

Directly back of the Supreme Court Building, or Old City Hall, at Fifth and Chestnut, stands the building of the American Philosophical Society. In architecture it is in style with the Independence Hall group, and is the only other building actually in the Square. The Philosophical Society's home was built just before the time of the meeting of the Constitutional Convention, and the Society still holds regular meetings in its quarters on the second and third floors. It was founded in 1743 by Benjamin Franklin, "a society," as he put it, "formed of virtuosi, or ingenious men residing in the several colonies," continuing, by amalgamation, the famous Junto he had originated in 1727, when he was only twenty-one years of age.

In 1769 the Society erected an observatory in the State House Yard, back of both its own building and the State House, for the purpose of observing the transit of Venus across the sun. These transits occur at intervals of about one hundred and five years, and from the observations the astronomers deduce the distance of the earth from the sun, which is "the yard-stick of the Universe." The Philadelphians had much more favorable weather than the European astronomers, and under the direction of David Rittenhouse the observations of the American Philosophical Society were regarded as the most reliable for the following century. At this observatory in the Yard were Dr. John Ewing, Joseph Shippen, Dr. Hugh Williamson, Thomas Pryor, Charles Thomson, and James Pearson; at Norriton were Rittenhouse, John Sellers, John Lukens, and Dr. William Smith, and at Henlopen Lighthouse, Owen Biddle.

South Orianna Street, once called Franklin Court, site of the home of Benjamin Franklin, where he wrote his autobiography, and where he died in 1790.

When Colonel Nixon read the Declaration of Independence to the people of Philadelphia assembled in the State House Yard, on July 8, 1776, he stood upon the platform of this observatory.

Now the oldest scientific institution in the United States, the American Philosophical Society has, as it always has had, an international reputation for distinguished membership. The first four presidents of the Society after the reorganization of 1768 were Franklin, Rittenhouse, Jefferson, and Wistar. Fifteen members of the Society were signers of the Declaration of Independence; eighteen members were framers of the Constitution of the United States. Eight members of the Society have become Presidents of the United States, and two other Presidents have become members. Twelve members of the Society have been Justices of the Supreme Court of the United States, and of these four were Chief Justices. All six of the Americans who have received the Nobel Prize were members of the American Philosophical Society. A large proportion of the scientists, publicists and scholars in the United States have been members of the Society, and the same is true of the more distinguished corresponding foreigners. The Society has a magnificent library and many other treasures, although not all can be kept in the building; these treasures include a Jefferson manuscript draft of the Declaration of Independence and about eighty per cent of the manuscripts of the writings of Franklin.

On the site of the rear of the Drexel Building, at Fifth and Sansom along the Square, was once the building of the Library Company of Philadelphia, "mother

The Franklin Institute, on Seventh Street north of Chestnut, the most notable memorial to Benjamin Franklin, scientist.

of all the North American subscription libraries,'' founded by Franklin in 1731, at one time housed in the State House wing, later in Carpenters' Hall, in 1789 in its own building at Fifth and Sansom, and about a century later finally housed in its present building on Locust Street near Broad. East on Chestnut Street, a block from our Square, and almost opposite Carpenters' Hall, is South Orianna Street, once called Franklin Court, where stood the house wherein Franklin completed his celebrated Autobiography, and wherein he died. In that Autobiography he relates that when he first came to Philadelphia, a youth of seventeen, he walked up High Street,—with a loaf of bread under his arm, you will remember,—as far as Fourth Street, and down Fourth to Chestnut, so passing within a few yards of the site of his last house.

Two blocks northward from the Square, at Fifth and Arch Streets, in Christ Church Cemetery, are the graves of Benjamin Franklin and his wife, Deborah, covered by a simple marble slab, close to a railed opening in the brick wall. Within four blocks westward from the Square are several other mementoes of his fame. On Seventh Street, around the northeast corner of Chestnut, is the century-old Franklin Institute, the activities of which include the encouragement of inventions, and the preservation, in a great library collection, of records of scientific research and progress. At Ninth and Chestnut, diagonally across from the new Benjamin Franklin Hotel,—whose electric sign flashes a portrait of the great electrician,—on the pavement of the building which now houses the Philadelphia Post Office, of

The grave of Benjamin Franklin, in Christ Church Cemetery, at Fifth and Arch Streets.

which he was once Postmaster, is a charming chaired statue of the man "venerated for benevolence, admired for talents, esteemed for patriotism, beloved for philanthropy."

Lower Chestnut Street

BUT to return to Independence Square. Rickett's Circus and the New Chestnut Street Theatre, of the capital city days of the late Eighteenth Century, have long since been removed; where the Circus was, is now the Public Ledger; and where the Theatre stood, is now the United Security Life Insurance and Trust Company; and where the Philadelphia Library Company had its first permanent home on Fifth Street, has long been the Drexel Building, home of the old Philadelphia banking house of the Drexels.

On the northeast corner of Fifth and Chestnut, diagonally across from the Old City Hall, is the Lafayette Building, named for the famous Frenchman by the estate of another. This building is the home of the Estate of Stephen Girard, "Mariner and Merchant," whose ship put into the port of Philadelphia in 1776, and who, when he discovered himself blockaded by British warships, decided to remain and enter business. When he died in 1831, after a long and useful life, he left the greatest American fortune of his time to found and endow Girard College. Robert Morris and Haym Salomon, financiers of the Revolutionary War; Stephen Girard and David Parish, financiers of the War of 1812; E. W. Clark, financier of the Mexican War; and Jay Cooke, financier of the Civil War, were all Philadelphians.

The Second Bank of the United States (1819–1824), now the Custom House, on Chestnut Street near Fifth. It is considered one of the finest specimens of Doric architecture in the world. From an old print.

Back of the Lafayette Building on Fifth Street, on the site of the Bourse, was once the Sparks Burial Ground of Seventh-Day Baptists. Richard Sparks was an early purchaser of lots in Philadelphia, and a member of the sect popularly known as Sabbath-Keepers, and in 1716 he willed this back-end of his High Street lot "for a burial place, for the use of the people or society called the Seventh-Day Baptists, forever." How it passed out of their use a hundred years later is a long story of contention between two congregations.

The Lafayette Building includes the offices of The Francis Perot's Sons Malting Company, which has the distinction of being the oldest existing business house in the country; it was founded in 1687, and is still conducted by a lineal descendant. In the same building are the offices of the John T. Lewis & Brothers Company, manufacturers of white lead, established in 1772, and still managed by members of the Lewis family. At 35 North Sixth, J. E. Rhoads & Sons still carry on the family leather business established in 1702. Within a block's walk of Independence Square are located the offices of a dozen or so business houses a century old or more.

On the south side of Chestnut Street, between Fourth and Fifth, is the United States Custom House, built in 1819 as the home of the second United States Bank. This structure was described by Charles Dickens as "a handsome building of white marble which had a mournful, ghost-like aspect dreary to behold. I attributed this to the sombre influence of the night, and on rising in the morning looked out again, expecting to

The Friends' Meeting House and School, once at Fourth and Chestnut Streets. The School is now called the William Penn Charter School. From an old print.

see its steps and portico thronged with groups of people passing in and out. The door was still tight-shut, however; the same cold, cheerless air prevailed, and the building looked as if the marble statue of Don Guzman could alone have any business to transact within its gloomy walls. I hastened to inquire its name and purpose, and then my surprise vanished. It was the tomb of many fortunes, the great catacomb of investment—the memorable United States Bank." A superb statue of Robert Morris now stands on the same steps.

On the east side of Fourth Street below Chestnut once stood the Friend's Meeting House, erected in 1763, and the Friends' Public School, which had been built some years earlier. This school had been chartered by William Penn, and now bears the name of the William Penn Charter School. After leaving Fourth Street it was located on Twelfth Street, between Market and Chestnut, up until very recently, and the Twelfth Street buildings still stand. Early in the eighteenth century there was a duck pond at Fourth and High Streets, which was the head of Dock Creek; and another duck pond, also famous for its shooting, was on the site of the present First Presbyterian Church, on Washington Square.

At 307 Chestnut Street is the modern home, on the original site, of the bank which, as the Bank of North America, was chartered in 1781, and, as now merged with the Commercial Trust Company, the union being known as the Bank of North America and Trust Company, is the oldest bank on the continent. It was organized by Robert Morris at a very critical period of

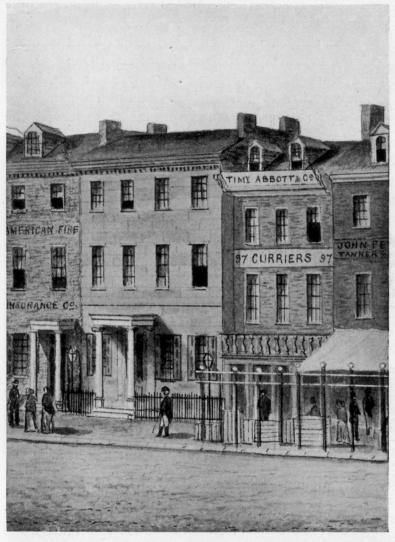

*The original home of the Bank of North America, oldest bank in America.
The building of the Bank of North America and Trust Company is on the
original site.   From an old water color.*

the Revolution, to support the credit of the Continental Congress. Chestnut Street, between Sixth and Second, is the traditional financial district of the City, although as a matter of fact there are quite a number of banks throughout another mile westward. Brown Brothers & Company, at Fourth and Chestnut, and the Philadelphia-Girard National Bank, at 421 Chestnut, are both centenarians. The latter had been the Philadelphia National Bank, which was organized in 1803, but in 1926 it joined with the Girard National Bank, under the new name. The Girard National Bank had grown out of the famous private Bank of Stephen Girard (1812-1832).

The First National Bank, of Philadelphia, at 315 Chestnut, was the first bank chartered under the National Banking Act of 1863. Its building is on the site of the Benezet House, the home of Anthony Benezet, a Friend celebrated in his day as an anti-slavery pamphleteer; he once leased his house to the Governor of Barbadoes, who used to come up Dock Creek by boat. The Benezet House had formerly been a public house under the name of the Hen and Chickens, and was eventually torn down to build the Franklin House.

Carpenters' Hall is in the back of the court which opens on Chestnut Street almost opposite Orianna Street. This building has interest entirely apart from the meeting of the First Continental Congress, for it is the hall of the Carpenters' Company, a guild in the ancient English sense, organized by the master carpenters of Philadelphia in the year 1724 "to obtain instruction in the science of architecture and to assist such of their

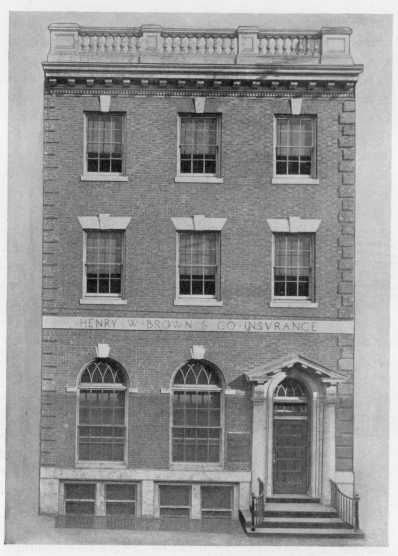

The insurance office of Henry W. Brown & Company, a modern building of Colonial architecture on Independence Square.

members as should be in need, as also their widows and minor children.'' Their hall was builded in 1770, and is in the form of a Greek cross. It has been used for many public purposes; it has housed both the first and the second Bank of the United States; it has been used as a custom house, as a library, as a hospital, and as a gunpowder magazine.

Around Independence Square

PERHAPS the most characteristic note in the business houses fronting on Independence Square is the use of bricks and marble in the Georgian or Colonial architecture, holding to the spirit of the State House Row. Two notable examples,- remarkable as highly successful in the experiment of adaptation in the case of such huge structures,—are the Curtis and Ledger Buildings, each covering a complete half of a city block. At the southeast corner of Fifth and Walnut is a third, that of the Independence Indemnity Company. Many of the other buildings, though of modern construction, cling, not only to Colonial architecture, but also to the Philadelphia tradition of housing a small company in a small building of its own rather than with dozens of other companies in a large building. And strikingly beautiful these business homes are, among them those of the United States Fidelity & Guaranty Company, Henry W. Brown & Company, Insurance; W. Frederick Snyder and Sydney L. Wright; the Home Life Insurance Company of America, Inc.; and George Wood, Sons & Company, and the Millville Manufacturing Company.

Fifth and Sansom Streets in the days when the Library Company of Philadelphia, the Mercantile Library, and the Philadelphia Dispensary had these three buildings along Fifth Street.

Of the two last-named companies, it may be added that the family has been manufacturing in the same location, at Millville, New Jersey, for one hundred and twenty-odd years.

William F. Murphy's Sons Company, Stationers, and the Pennsylvania Fire Insurance Company, are two more century-old businesses housed on Independence Square; and at 517 Chestnut the Pennsylvania Company for Insurances on Lives and Granting Annuities, founded 1812, uses as a branch office what was long its main office and is now the banking building of the Real Estate Title Insurance & Trust Company of Philadelphia, the oldest title insurance company in the world, although founded only in the Centennial year.

At the south corner of Fifth and Sansom, on the Square, is the original columned home of the Mercantile Library, now occupied by the Philadelphia News Bureau. On the other corner had formerly been the Library Company of Philadelphia, and because of these two buildings this stretch of Sansom Street was once called Library Street; it is still so marked. Next door to the Mercantile Library stood until recently the Philadelphia Dispensary, the first of its kind in the country, established in 1786, and here built in 1801. For over a century it ministered freely to sick and injured poor applicants. At the southeast corner of Sixth and Walnut is the white granite building of The Penn Mutual Life Insurance Company (chartered 1847) forming, with the Curtis Building on the northwest corner, a canyon-pass through which blow the winds of Independence Square into Washington Square.

In Washington Square to-day.

Washington Square

ON THAT great checker-board of the map of a Philadelphia to reach from South to Vine Street, and from River to River, William Penn's surveyor-general had marked off five squares as dedicated to the use of the public by the Proprietor and Governor. Of those five squares one was "the Southeast Square," long after named for Washington, as the other four also came to be named for Colonial celebrities,—Penn, Logan, Franklin, and Rittenhouse. So that Washington Square is almost a century older than its venerable neighbor, Independence Square. Within two decades of the landing of Penn's Quakers, the Southeast Square was being used as the potters' field, and, as we have seen, it supplied a final resting place for many other than the poor and the strangers. Although there is not a headstone in the Square, there is one marker; a rough-hewn stone with a simple bronze plate to remind passers-by of the soldiers who sleep there.

To-day Washington Square is a pleasant green spot, with well-kept lawns and shrubs and flag-stoned walks shaded by a variety of trees. A few of these, giants of height and dignity, are relics of a day when the place was a pet charge of arborists, who had planted four hundred trees of fifty varieties. Of the modern plantings, perhaps the most interesting is the row of young ginkgo trees used as a curbstone border; for the ginkgo is comparatively seldom seen, and has this curious distinction, that it is older than any other native growing thing in America. The ginkgo was a native of America and

The Farm Journal Building at the southwest corner of Washington Square.

Asia, and was annihilated in America during the Glacial Age; the modern ginkgo of America is an importation from China, but it has an American "family tree" just about as old as the Neanderthal Man.

Washington Square has long been Philadelphia's centre for publishing businesses. Facing the Square are J.B. Lippincott Company, the Catholic Standard & Times, David McKay, the W. B. Saunders Company, the Central News Co., the Farm Journal, and Lea & Febiger. These are all long established. The last-named, in its new white stone building, continues the business of Matthew Carey, established in 1785 and partly financed by a loan from Lafayette. It is the oldest book publishing business in the country, and incidentally publishes a magazine over a century old, the American Journal of the Medical Sciences. The Lippincott business was established in 1792. At the corner of Seventh and Walnut Streets is the Pennsylvania Bible Society; founded in 1808, it is the oldest in the country. As the Atlantic Agency of the American Bible Society, which was instituted in 1816, it distributes Bibles printed in seventy-three different languages.

These Washington Square publishing houses have a fame which reaches far afield. The Farm Journal and the Country Gentleman keep in constant touch with rural districts all over the country. The varied catalogue of Lippincott books has a national reputation, as have the text-books of Lea & Febiger and the illustrated volumes published by David McKay. The medical books of the W. B. Saunders Company, and the Saturday Evening Post and the Ladies Home Journal of the Curtis

The W. B. Saunders Company Building on Washington Square.

Publishing Company, have a truly world-wide fame.

Few visitors leave this neighborhood without going into the Curtis Building to see the mural decoration of The Dream Garden, the magnificent Maxfield Parrish painting translated into a fifty-foot favrile glass mosaic by Louis C. Tiffany.

On Washington Square is another "first":—The Philadelphia Savings Fund Society at Walnut Street and West Washington Square, was founded in 1816 as a benevolent institution without stockholders. At 219 South Sixth is a building of Italian Renaissance architecture, erected in 1847,—the Athenaeum Library, organized as a reading room in 1814, and continuing with a membership which is practically hereditary. In the same east row is Fire Company No. 32, "least quiet in a quiet Square."

On South Washington Square at Seventh Street is the First Presbyterian Church, here built just a century ago, although its congregation had been formed as early as 1692, building the first Presbyterian church (1704) on High Street, in a grove of buttonwood trees. The great Corinthian columns from the second "Old Buttonwood" (1794) were used in the stately portico of the present First Presbyterian Church, the interior of which also has many charming features. Through the congregation of this church and the Philadelphia Presbytery and Synod came the foundation of Princeton College.

The W. B. Saunders Company, the American Gas Company, and the J. B. Lippincott Company, all at Locust Street corners of Washington Square, and the

Southwest from Washington Square, showing the First Presbyterian Church, and the Orange Street Friends' Meeting House on the site of the present Farm Journal Building.

Farm Journal, have handsome brick modern buildings in the Colonial style. In front of the Farm Journal Building,—part of which is on the site of the old Orange Street Friends' Meeting House,—there is a pleasant evergreen garden, extending around what is almost the only left-angle street corner in the city. Nearby, on the south side of the Square, is a group of century-old brick houses, two of which now house the Christopher Morley Inn. The inn is the center of a quiet art colony whose studios are to be found on Washington Square and in its vicinity.

At 245 South Sixth Street is an old house which, between 1818 and 1824, was the residence of General Count Grouchy, the man upon whose failure to carry out the spirit of his orders the Emperor Napoleon attributed his defeat at Waterloo. After Napoleon's downfall, the feeling against Count Grouchy was strong enough to cause him to leave France and come to Philadelphia, where he found Joseph Bonaparte, brother of Napoleon and himself ex-King of Spain, established at the Potter house at 260 South Ninth Street. The little group of expatriated Bonapartists, like the royalist *emigres* of the French Revolution before them, and the Jacobins as well, often met at the democratic board of Stephen Girard, the French-born merchant.

A block southwest from Washington Square is the country's oldest hospital, The Pennsylvania, chartered in 1751. The original building was erected in 1755 and is still in use; its cornerstone has this inscription by Franklin: "In the year of Christ MDCCLV, George the

The Pine Street front of the Pennsylvania Hospital. From an old engraving on steel, by Tucker.

Second happily reigning (for he sought the happiness of his people) Philadelphia flourishing (for its inhabitants were publick spirited) this building, by the bounty of the government and of many private persons, was piously founded for the relief of the sick and miserable; may the God of Mercies bless the undertaking."

Franklin was the first secretary, the second president and one of the staunchest supporters of the originator, Dr. Thomas Bond. At the time of the foundation, few hospitals already existed, and they were in the principal cities of Europe. The views expressed in the wording of the petition for the establishment of the Pennsylvania Hospital, especially in behalf of "the distempered in mind," were far in advance of the times. Though prior to that time confinement of lunatics in cells or dungeons was largely resorted to, thenceforth insanity was recognized as a disease. This was forty years before the movements in England and France for that recognition and for systematic medical treatment in hospitals.

The old hospital buildings are still in use, together with modern structures, within a Colonial brick wall, occupying the whole block from Pine to Spruce and from Eighth to Ninth Streets, and the services rendered through the successive generations have given to the Pennsylvania Hospital a world-wide reputation and have made its records valuable in the medical libraries of all countries and its clinical instruction much sought. Since 1841 the insane department has been located in the group of buildings in West Philadelphia which are popularly known as "Kirkbride's."

It was probably the main location of the old hospital

REBECCA GRATZ
BORN MARCH 4 1781 DIED AUGUST 27 1869

The Portuguese and Spanish Hebrew burial ground of Congregation Mikve Israel, and the back of the Pennsylvania Hospital, across Spruce Street.

which has been responsible for the popularity of Spruce Street as a community of residences and offices for almost a thousand physicians.

Across from the hospital, on Spruce Street, is a brick-walled graveyard which was consecrated in 1740— the cemetery of the Congregation Mikve Israel, who were Spanish and Portuguese Jews. Herein is buried Rebecca Gratz, who, as pictured by Scott from the description of Washington Irving, was the original of Rebecca in "Ivanhoe." The first Israelites in Philadelphia were descendants of families expelled from Spain by the edict of Ferdinand and Isabella, and it is said that there were Jews in Pennsylvania before the landing of Penn.

All through this old hospital neighborhood, and especially on Spruce Street between Fourth and Eighth, are greatly admired Colonial homes; and the section is constantly visited by architects studying the effects and details of the doorways, steps, foot scrapers, knockers, and railings. The best known of this scattered colony of old houses is the Morris House, at 225 South Eighth Street, with its gardens.

Just off Washington Square, on the south side of Prune (now Locust) Street between Fifth and Sixth, a converted warehouse was used, between 1820 and 1825, as a playhouse known as the Winter Tivoli or Prune Street Theatre. Here also was the original location of Jefferson Medical College, now over a century old.

Before leaving Washington Square we are reminded that part of the Walnut Street ground of the Curtis Building was the site of the Loganian Library, there

The Independence Indemnity Company's Building on Independence Square.

established in 1790, in which were deposited the great collection of rare books eventually bequeathed to the Library Company of Philadelphia by Chief Justice James Logan, of Stenton. Before the publishing building was erected, the old houses fronting on Walnut Street were called Lawyers' Row, having long been used as offices by lawyers wishing to be convenient to the courts then held in State House Row, around the corner.

The Insurance District

WALNUT Street, from Washington Square to Dock Street, has long been the insurance district of Philadelphia. Beginning at Sixth Street, eastward (toward the Delaware River) almost every building on both sides of Walnut Street is occupied with offices of insurance companies and agencies, and as Walnut Street meets the cross streets the district bulges out a block or so both north and south. Many of these companies and agencies, most of them in fact, are long established, and among the general run of buildings of average age, with here and there a fine new building, occasionally a company or an agency has taken over some very old house and converted it into offices, so that a visitor entering a perhaps dingy building is surprised to come upon a beautiful staircase, or a graceful fanlight, or a room wherein doors, fireplace, and windows are connected by white wooden panelling into the definite architectural scheme of an early Colonial house, or where there is the massive walnut woodwork of a later period.

The Penn Mutual Building, from Independence Square.

The insurance district has a personality distinctive to itself in Philadelphia. To a large extent this is due to the peculiarities of the insurance business, which requires the constant inter-relation of the companies and agencies, what with the underwriting of an interminable line of insurances,—life, fire, marine, accident, health, automobile, casualty, plate glass, burglary, liability, workmen's compensation, property damage, collision, earthquake, hail, cyclone, tornado, and so on indefinitely. This underwriting and reinsurance work created the insurance district, and it keeps together these business houses in a town within the city, and of course it promotes a community spirit and fellowship which form and maintain traditions.

The men and women of the insurance district,—one might almost say of the whole Independence Square neighborhood,—have their own luncheon and meeting places. To them Bookbinder's Restaurant, Hammill's Oyster Cellar, the Bourse Cafeteria, Wiener's Restaurant, the Girard Buffet, are landmarks,—almost clubs. They set their watches by the curious old clock in the window of the Liverpool and London and Globe Building, with thirteen dials telling the corresponding time at Philadelphia, London, Paris, Berlin, Constantinople, St. Petersburg, Calcutta, Hong Kong, Melbourne, New Orleans, Chicago, Valparaiso, and New York; although they no longer cheer the arrival of noon as indicated by the dropping of the great silver ball on the roof of the Bourse, for the ships on the river now are signalled the time by radio. The people of the insurance district know the arresting beauty of the two Squares on a

The building of the Philadelphia Contributionship, on South Fourth Street. It was erected in 1835 to serve as the Hand-in-Hand Office and also as the home of the Secretary-Treasurer, so that he might live on the premises to guard the securities.

winter's morning before the snow has melted from the boughs; they judge when spring has actually arrived, not by Poor Richard's Almanac any longer, but by the leafing of those trees; and they know the magic in the old lamp reflections on the flagstones, on a rainy night, as they hurry through Independence Square on the way to a late train for commuters.

Another influence in the insurance district is the historical one, for some of these businesses have their roots deep in that historical ground, and there is the frequent reminder, in site and relic, of the Colonial period when the Independence Square neighborhood, particularly to the east and southeast, was half the city. There are ancient churches and houses, and here and there a curious byway, more of London than of Philadelphia,—a Walnut Place, a Franklin Court, a Willing's Alley, a Custom House Place, a Dock Street.

Of the companies long established in the insurance district, the oldest is the Philadelphia Contributionship for the Insurance of Houses from Loss by Fire, located at 212 South Fourth Street. It was organized in 1752 and is the oldest fire insurance company in America. Since 1835 it has been in this quaint old house, with a beautiful garden, wherein the Secretary-Treasurer was required to live, in those days before the time of safe deposit companies, as custodian of the securities. One of its treasures is the fifteen foot parchment scroll of The Articles of Association, signed by over 1700 earlier members of the Contributionship, the second name being that of the ubiquitous Benjamin Franklin. The fire mark of this company is four hands united,—the

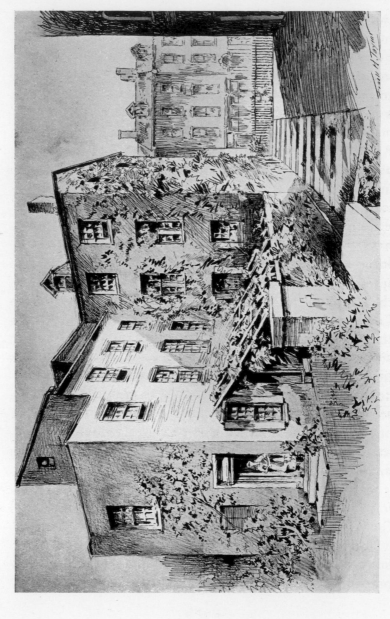

The garden of the Green Tree fire insurance office, the Cadwalader and Wistar houses. On the left is the parent vine of the Wistaria. On the right is the churchyard of St. Mary's.

Hand-in-Hand, and its badges were originally made by John Pass, of Pass & Stow, of Liberty Bell fame.

Franklin was interested, not only in this first fire insurance company, but the city's first fire-fighting company as well. And he almost founded life insurance in Philadelphia, but his suggestion was a little premature. Life insurance did not get really started in America until 1843, and in its modern form only dates back to 1706, in London, although it has been traced in its origin as far back as Roman times. But that is another story.

When the Hand-in-Hand ruled that "No Houses having a Tree or Trees planted before them shall be Insured or Re-Insured" because trees were thought to spread fire and hamper fire-fighting, forty members of the Contributionship organized the Mutual Assurance Company to insure houses whether trees were near them or not. That was in 1784, and the new company adopted the Green Tree fire mark as the sign of its liberality. Its success quickly demonstrated the Philadelphians' determination to keep a green as well as a red city. A graceful tradition at the monthly dinner of the Board of Trustees of the Green Tree is a standing toast to George Washington, continued from a monthly dinner of 1799 when news came of his death.

Both these companies sell "perpetual insurance," a form which is peculiar to Philadelphia, Baltimore, and Cincinnati.

Many people who see fire marks on old buildings do not realize that these quaint badges once had a genuinely practical purpose, which was to enable the volunteer

Four famous Philadelphia fire marks: the Hand-in-Hand, the Green Tree, the Eagle, and the Hydrant-and-Hose. From " Fire Insurance House Marks of the United States," by Gillespie and Walsh.

fire brigades, to whose support the insurance companies contributed, to know which houses it would be their duty especially to protect. The firemen upon arriving at a blaze first looked to see if the house had the proper fire mark; if it had not, the probability was that the fire hazard was increased. The old fire insurance companies were frequently better known by the names of their fire marks than by their corporate names. In Philadelphia there have been fire marks of eight different local insurance companies, and these badges of the days of volunteer fire-fighting may be seen on the fronts of dozens of the buildings throughout this section of the city, although in most sections of Philadelphia fire marks are now a rarity.

In many of the insurance offices a visitor will see collections of Philadelphia and foreign fire marks, along with curious paraphernalia of the old volunteer fire companies, quaint and colorful relics of a day when fire-fighting was quite as much a matter of fighting as it was of fire. But that, too, is another story.

At Fourth and Walnut Streets is the building of the Fire Association of Philadelphia, which was instituted in 1817 "to promote harmony and friendly intercourse and to establish those just relations which ought to exist among institutions having similar views; the undersigned engine and hose companies have formed themselves into an Association to be styled The Fire Association of Philadelphia." There were eleven of these fire, and five hose, companies in The Fire Association, the oldest of which had been instituted in 1742. Its fire mark was the Hydrant-and-Hose.

St. Joseph's Roman Catholic Church, hidden away in Willing's Alley, south of Walnut Street, and between Third and Fourth Streets. From a photographic study by John Allen.

In 1792 The Insurance Company of North America, oldest joint stock company in America, was organized in the Declaration Chamber of Independence Hall; it is using as a branch office at Third and Walnut what was until recently its home office. The I. C. N. A. fire mark was the Eagle.

The Insurance Company of the State of Pennsylvania, at 308 Walnut Street, was organized in 1794. At 510 Walnut Street is another centenarian, The Pennsylvania Fire Insurance Company, founded 1825.

The Old Churches

SEVERAL of the churches of the Revolutionary period still survive throughout this insurance locality, but in most cases business buildings have pressed so close upon them as to have occasioned the statement that "the city of churches hides its old churches." The most completely hidden place of worship is St. Joseph's Roman Catholic Church, in Willing's Alley, on the north side, between Third and Fourth Streets. The present building is the fourth of the name, occupying the site of the first, where the Catholic Church was founded in Philadelphia in 1733, the first congregation comprising twenty-two Irish and fifteen Germans.

It was at St. Joseph's that Longfellow's poem is usually taken to have had Evangeline and Gabriel buried; "Side by side, in their nameless graves, the lovers are sleeping, under the humble walls of the little Catholic churchyard." And a few doors below on Willing's Alley is an entrance to Walnut Place, wherein

St. Paul's Church building on South Fourth Street, built in 1762; now a city mission. Edwin Forrest, the tragedian, is buried in the churchyard near the entrance.

was once the Quaker Almshouse where Evangeline found her long-lost lover. But the people of the neighborhood take the poetic fiction so seriously that they argue that of course Evangeline was buried in the vault of the nursing sisterhood to which she belonged, at the Catholic Church of the Holy Trinity, at Sixth and Spruce Streets, where the communicants were mostly Germans and French,—for it was established (1789) for German Catholics and was, in fact, the first exclusively national church in America. The presence of the exiled Acadians, "the French Neutrals," was no fiction; over four hundred of them were sent to Philadelphia from Nova Scotia because they had refused to take the oath of allegiance to Great Britain; they were provided with quarters in a row of one-story wooden houses built on the north side of Pine Street between Fifth and Sixth, and a number of them found their final resting place in the potters' field of Washington Square.

Across the street from Holy Trinity Church is the house wherein Joseph Jefferson was born, so that within three blocks along Spruce Street we find three famous but strangely assorted neighbors,—Rip Van Winkle, Evangeline, and Rebecca of Ivanhoe.

St. Mary's, at Fourth above Spruce, was the second Roman Catholic Church in the city; it was built 1763, and became the cathedral church when the first Catholic bishop of Philadelphia, Right Reverend Michael Egan, O. S. F., was appointed. The first French Minister to the United States, Chevalier Gerard, and his suite attended services at St. Mary's, and it was at his request that at this church was held the first public religious

The Prune Street Theatre, once on Locust Street below Sixth; where "Home Sweet Home" was introduced to American singing.

celebration of the Declaration, July 4, 1779, with the Continental Congress attending the Te Deum. In the graveyard is the tomb of Commodore Barry, father of the American Navy, whose statue is to be seen in Independence Square.

Old Pine Street Presbyterian Church is on the southwest corner of Fourth and Pine. Built in 1768, it is the only Presbyterian building preserved from the Colonial period. John Adams, during his presidency, was a communicant. St. Peter's, on the southeast corner of Third and Pine, was dedicated in 1761, and was long united with Christ Church, sharing its rectors, among whom were Jacob Duché and Bishop White. Washington had a pew in both churches. In the church-yard of St. Peter's is a monument to Commodore Stephen Decatur. St. Paul's, built in 1762, on Third Street below Walnut, has become the Philadelphia Protestant Epis-copal City Mission. The tragedian, Edwin Forrest, is buried in a tomb to the right of the entrance.

There are two other churches, perhaps the most celebrated of all, just outside the neighborhood, but still so near that we must not pass them by. On Swanson Street, near Front and Christian, is Old Swedes' Church, "Gloria Dei," the oldest church building in Philadel-phia, dedicated in 1700, on a site used by the early Swedes for religious services since 1677. And on Second Street above Market is Christ Church. Built in 1727 on grounds acquired for church purposes in 1702 by a congregation dating from 1695, Christ Church is quite as famous for its architecture as for its historic signifi-cance. It was designed by Dr. John Kearsley, a lay archi-

The first Chestnut Street Theatre, built in 1793, burned down in 1820, rebuilt in 1822, and torn down in 1855. "Hail, Columbia" was first sung here in 1798. A Birch print, 1800.

tect, and Christ Church and Independence Hall (which also was designed by a lay architect) have had a gentle but powerful influence on the popularity of Colonial architecture throughout the city and its environs.

Visitors from out of town, thinking of old Philadelphia as "the Quaker City," often express surprise when they learn of the early dates of foundation of these various churches of different denominations. But as a matter of fact the Friends were in the ascendency for only the first seventy-five years. And it should be remembered that when Penn sought his grant of land he declared and sincerely intended that "the first fundamental of the government in my province shall be that everyone shall have and enjoy free possession of his faith and exercise of worship in such way and manner as every such person shall in conscience believe most acceptable to God." Mere toleration did not satisfy Penn; he made religious liberty a right. "We must give the liberty we ask." Although after Penn's departure Pennsylvania did recede somewhat from his broad ground of religious freedom, due largely to the influence of the home government, so that there were for a time certain restrictions, nevertheless Penn's principle won out, and with the success of St. Joseph's came "the triumph of religious liberty."

Romantic Houses

BUT the insurance district has other famous historical as well as church and business associations with early days.

*Still standing at Fourth and Walnut Streets: the Stephen Moylan house on the corner,
and the Dolly Madison house to the north (left).*

There is an old brick house at the northeast corner of Fourth and Walnut, the first floor of which is now occupied by a cigar store. This old house was once the home of General Stephen Moylan, of Washington's staff, first Commissioner of Pensions, and first President of the Friendly Sons of St. Patrick. The house next door on Fourth Street, which looks as though it might be a wing of the Moylan house, was the home of Dorothea Payne at the time her first husband died, and it was probably in this house that she met "the great little Madison," who was presented by Aaron Burr. As Dolly Madison she became perhaps the most celebrated mistress of the White House.

The boarding house wherein died Chief Justice John Marshall, in 1835, was on Walnut Street, below Fourth. It was while tolling during his funeral services that the Liberty Bell cracked.

At the southwest corner of Third and Walnut Streets once stood "Fort Wilson," the home of James Wilson, signer of the Declaration. The house was stormed by a mob one autumn day in 1779 because he had, as a lawyer at the State House, defended Tories accused of treason during the British occupation of the town. Wilson and his friends valiantly defended the "Fort" until the Philadelphia Troop of Light Horse came and dispersed the rioters. Mention of the old military may serve to remind that not far from here, at Water Street and Tun Alley, between Walnut and Chestnut Streets, was the Tun Tavern, which witnessed the organization of the United States Marine Corps, when, the Continental Congress, November 10, 1775,

The Indian Queen, on South Fourth Street. Next door to the north (left) was Francis' Hotel, and one door more the office of the New York stage coach. From a Smith Ale print.

having authorized the formation of the Corps, the first recruiting station was opened at the tavern.

At the southwest corner of Fourth and Locust Streets still stands the Wistar House, wherein lived Dr. Caspar Wistar, physician and scientist, in whose honor after his death a group of his friends of the American Philosophical Society originated the Wistar Parties, a distinctively Philadelphia social institution something in the nature of a salon; in the beginning membership in the Society was a requirement by the Parties. Both the Wistar House and the Cadwalader House, next door, are occupied by the Green Tree. In the garden is the original of the Wistaria vine, named for Dr. Wistar by Michaux, the great botanist.

On the northwest corner once was the house wherein lived Louis Philippe, later King of the French.

The Indian Queen, an inn of the late eighteenth century, was on Fourth Street, on the east side, below Market, on the site of the Daly automobile agency. It is possible that the present building may have been the inn, despite its alterations, for it is a very old structure of red bricks and black-headers. Next door, to the north, was Francis' Hotel, and at both houses lived a number of the national statesmen of the time, including both John Adams and Thomas Jefferson. The Francis Hotel was the scene of the famous incident after the inauguration of President Adams, when Washington, accompanied by Timothy Pickering, walked from Congress Hall down Chestnut Street, with a great crowd following, and called to pay his respects to the new chief executive.

The forerunner of all bank buildings in America—built as the First Bank of the United States in 1797, from 1812 to 1832 the private Bank of Stephen Girard, then the Girard Bank, and finally, until very recently, the Girard National Bank.   The building still stands, at Third and Dock Streets.   From a Birch print.

The Powel Mansion, on the west side of Third Street below Walnut, still stands; the home of Samuel Powel, first Mayor of Philadelphia under the new United States, two of whose most frequent guests were President Washington and Vice President John Adams. Another ancient house, at Second and Walnut, is the Old Krider Gun Shop, on the spot where was born the first white child in Philadelphia, 1680.

On Second Street above Walnut was the location of the City Tavern, perhaps the most celebrated of all the Colonial inns. And here at Second and Walnut, near the northeast corner of Gray's Alley, was once a watch-maker whose apprentice was that Robert Fulton who invented and builded the steamboat Clermont. It will be recalled that John Fitch first applied steam to naviga-tion in Philadelphia in 1785. A balance wheel from his vessel is in Congress Hall.

Around the corner, on Third Street facing Dock Street, is the oldest bank building in the country, a handsome, mellowed white marble building with a portico of great Corinthian columns, built in 1795 for Alexander Hamilton's first Bank of the United States, and later used as the private Bank of Stephen Girard. Another old building, at the end of Dock Street, is that of the Merchant's Exchange, the growth of which can be traced to the meetings of traders in the old City Tavern. The building was once occupied by the Stock Exchange.

In such a stolidly planned city as Philadelphia, the winding Dock Street is come upon somewhat unex-pectedly. This picturesque market-place is the center of

Dock Creek and the Blue Anchor Tavern, about 1700. Where William Penn landed in Philadelphia.

traffic in the city's food supplies, the wholesale pro-
vision warehouses and markets;—and, by the way, at
the nearby Second Street Market, at Pine Street, (the
"New Market") business has gone on uninterruptedly
since 1745, when it catered to the fashionable neighborhood of that day. A number of the old Dock Street
buildings have but recently been torn down to make
way for the Seaman's Church Institute, a modern
structure devoted to the welfare of seamen in port.
There is a certain poetic justice in that, for Dock Street
was once Dock Creek, running into the Delaware River.
Seagoing vessels in the early days entered the creek to
dock and to obtain fresh water from nearby springs.
It was arriving at the public dock which gave the creek
its name that William Penn landed in Philadelphia.
The Blue Anchor Inn, the town's first public house,
was at Dock Creek, on the west side of Front Street,
and Penn's party were its guests. The old creek was
covered over about the year 1785, and still remains one
of the several legendary "underground rivers" of the
city. One of its tributaries which ran through Washington Square at one time still causes trouble to engineers
when it is rediscovered while they are digging for
foundations of new buildings.

At 227 on Dock Street was once the office of Edgar
Allan Poe, at a time when he was editing Burton's
Gentleman's Magazine. Not far away were once two
houses associated with the founder of Pennsylvania; at
Second Street, on the southeast corner of Norris's Alley,
was the Slate Roof House, occupied by William Penn,
and wherein was born his son John,—"John, the Ameri-

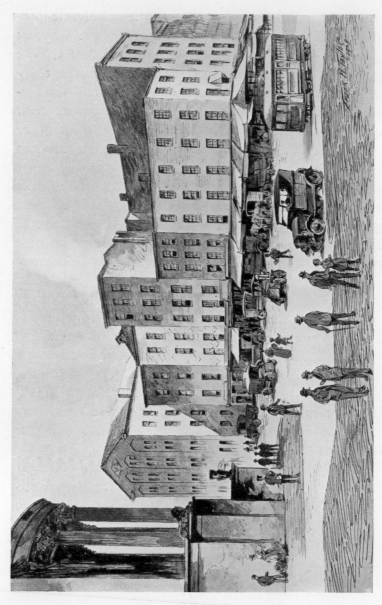

The markets of Dock Street where it crosses Walnut Street, with the Merchants' Exchange Building to the left, as they looked a decade ago.

can;" and in Letitia Court, near Market, William Penn builded the Letitia House as his Philadelphia home. It was this tiny house that was finally moved out to Fairmount Park, where you may still see it, "the first State House in the Province of Pennsylvania."

Which brings us back to the subject of the most famous State House, Independence Hall, and to the personages and events identified with State House Row.

Jos. N. Pearce.

State House Row from Independence Square, looking toward the northeast. Congress Hall on the extreme left, then the West Wing and Arcade, Independence Hall, the East Arcade and Wing, the Supreme Court Building, and the American Philosophical Society Building.

STATE HOUSE ROW

Independence Hall

T HE Independence Hall group comprises Independence Hall, two arcades connecting it with two small two-story buildings called the wings, and the two larger buildings, the one on the corner of Fifth Street, known as the Supreme Court Building, and the one on the Sixth Street corner, known as Congress Hall. The group still is usually called State House Row, for Independence Hall was originally the State House of the Province of Pennsylvania; the Supreme Court Building was the City Hall; and Congress Hall was the County Building.

Philadelphia in the early days being the headquarters of the Province,—indeed the only town approaching the size of a city,—and the Provincial Assembly of Pennsylvania having been compelled to "hire a house annually" in which to meet, the necessity of a House of the Assembly was considered, and it was "unanimously resolved that £2,000 of the £30,000 to be emitted in paper currency should be appropriated toward building such a House." This was in 1729, and the next year, the committee appointed having selected the

How the State House looked in 1778—painted by Charles Willson Peale as a background detail of his portrait of M. Gerard, now in Independence Hall. When the portrait was cleaned, a few years ago, this was rediscovered.

south side of Chestnut Street between Fifth and Sixth Streets as a site, began to buy up the ground.

In the spring of 1732 ground was broken and the building begun. Andrew Hamilton, a member of that committee and a prominent lawyer of the town, designed the edifice and carried out its construction. While his work had to do only with the State House and its arcades and wings, he recognized the future requirements of both city and county for accommodations, so he created a trust in the Fifth and Sixth Street corners of the ground, planning that city and county buildings should eventually be erected there in such design and size as to bring the whole facade into one general effect. Although the city and county buildings were not begun until half a century later, the originator's dream was finally realized.

The building of the State House seems to have been an adventure in architecture, with the original plan gracefully giving way to the tendency to develop the first idea. Some idea of the delays and alterations may be seen from the statement that "the State House was practically completed in 1759,"—after a quarter of a century's work.

The changes which occasionally took place after the Colonial Period were apparently never in the interests of architectural improvement; they were made for utility's greater aid or for reasons of economy in replacement.

The first occupancy of the State House by the Legislature of Pennsylvania was in October, 1736, although the building operations were far from complete. It is

Independence Hall—a winter's night.

interesting to know that the Speaker of that Assembly, and hence the first presiding officer of the room of the Declaration and of the Constitution, was Andrew Hamilton, the designer and builder of the Hall; and the Clerk of the Assembly was Benjamin Franklin.

In viewing the exterior of Independence Hall one observes that while the brick Chestnut Street front is ornamented with white stone quoins, band courses, keystones and panels, it yet remains severe in effect as compared with the southern front, where the builder's economy caused the omission of the decorative stone-work. This effect, of course, is due to the addition, on the southern or Square front, of the great brick tower, breaking the straight line of the rectangle; and there is the lovely Palladian window above the tower door.

When you come into Independence Hall, on the right, as you enter the hallway, three large arches between columns open into the Judicial Chamber, while on the left are closed arches and a doorway leading into the east room, which was intended for the Provincial Assembly. Before you is an arched entrance to the tower, with its splendid stairway, Palladian window, and door into the Square. The hallway and rooms on the ground floor are designed in English Renaissance, decorated in white wainscoting, "with pilasters which, with strict classic propriety, are of the Doric order on the first floor, progressing to Ionic on the stair landing and to the Corinthian cornice beneath the tower ceiling. The details throughout are dignified and massive, corresponding to the classic proportions that governed the design of wooden as well as stone architecture of the period."

The Judicial or State Supreme Court Chamber, in Independence Hall.

The second floor is divided so as to provide a full length gallery across the front, with three apartments in back, of which the center one serves as a vestibule from the stair hall, while the room to the right was the Governor's Room, and that to the left was a Council Room. The long gallery was the Banquet Hall, which, incidentally, was used as a hospital for wounded American officers after the Battle of Germantown. These rooms of the second floor are now used to exhibit an excellent collection of portraits of Colonial patriots. Many of these were painted by Charles Willson Peale, who had in 1802 opened in the Banquet Hall what was probably the first museum in America; this portrait group was in that original museum collection, which had also included birds, insects, fishes, minerals, and fossils.

In the west room of the first floor, which was the Judicial Chamber, the Supreme Court of Pennsylvania held its sessions. The convention to form a new Constitution for Pennsylvania met here in 1776, from July to September, and during its meetings unanimously approved the Declaration of Independence. In the Council Chamber, in 1771, there was at least one grand talk with the Indians. Chiefs of the Cayugas, of the Delawares, Shawanese, Tuscaroras, and Mohicans were present; they came on a friendly visit to confirm the lands delivered to Onas, as they called William Penn. (An Indian pun—Onas meant Quill). Deputations from different Indian tribes frequently came to treat with the Provisional Government. They were entertained in the State House Yard, and sometimes lodged in one of

A conjectural sketch of the whole city of Philadelphia about the year 1707. Dock Creek may plainly be seen, with its pond at Fourth and High Streets, and its dock and mouth in the left foreground; also the high river banks in which the first settlers dug their caves. About the left half of this picture shows what developed into the Independence Square Neighborhood. From a print at the Historical Society of Pennsylvania.

the Wings. The long, low sheds on the Fifth and Sixth Street corners of the Yard, at Chestnut Street, which preceded the City and County Buildings, were erected as quarters for Indian deputations; during the Revolution these sheds were used for artillery and munitions of war.

Independence Hall was abandoned as a State House in 1799, when Lancaster was made the temporary seat of the Commonwealth of Pennsylvania, and thereafter Harrisburg was made the permanent state capital. The reason for the transfer was simply to secure a location nearer the center of the state.

Philadelphia, by purchase, became the owner of the Hall in 1816. The City made no notable use of it, but the visit and reception of Lafayette, in 1824, drew public attention to the building and a partial restoration was a result. It was not until 1876, the Centennial year, that the Hall was relieved of its accumulation of miscellaneous museum collections and of certain architectural additions.

The Centennial restoration, with its recognition of the good taste of the Colonial builders, paved the way for a general interest in the beauties dictated by that good taste. During the past two decades, under the patriotic direction of the experts of the Philadelphia Chapter of the American Institute of Architecture, Independence Hall has been restored to that graceful appearance it had during those stirring days of the Revolution when its stately and dignified charm provided a noble setting for the deliberations of the troubled fathers of the new nation.

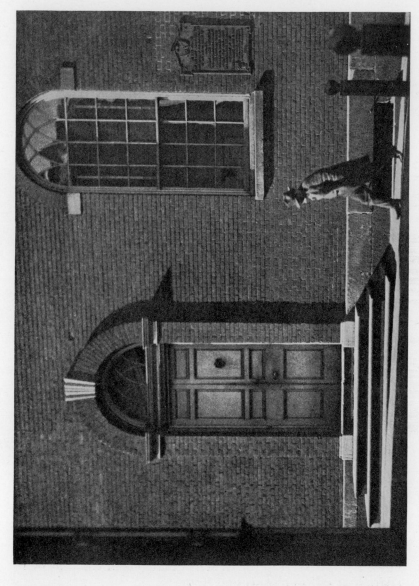

The east door of Congress Hall, as seen from the west wing of Independence Hall.

From a photograph made by A. J. Carson.

Another extraordinary event occurred in Independence Hall as recently as 1918, when a congress of Czecho-Slovakians met in the Banquet Room to frame the Declaration of Independence of the twelve states of the Democratic Mid-European Union. These representatives of sixty-five million people oppressed by German, Austrian, and Ottoman rule, signed their Declaration on October 26, 1918, in the original Declaration Chamber, and in Independence Square proclaimed their freedom with a Liberty Bell of their own—demonstrating the profound and world-wide influence of the sentiment of Independence Hall.

State House Row now houses a National Museum, a permanent public exhibition of early American portraiture and a general collection of objects associated with the history of America from the period of discovery on up to the middle of the last century. In the main corridor of Independence Hall, at the tower entrance, is the greatest treasure, the Liberty Bell; and because visitors have so often been prevented from seeing it, by reason of arriving after open hours, two panels in the tower door have been replaced with glass and the corridor illuminated all night long, so that the Bell may be seen from outside. In the Declaration Chamber are articles of the original furniture used by the Continental Congress and the Constitutional Convention, including the "rising sun" chair and desk, and the splendid silver inkwell used by "the Signers." Also in Independence Hall is the National Portrait Gallery of Colonial patriots, statesmen, and officers, for the most part housed on the second floor.

Congress Hall, at the southeast corner of Sixth and Chestnut Streets, and at the western end of State House Row in Independence Square.

In the two wings of Independence Hall, and in Congress Hall and the Supreme Court Building, are the collections of art, relics, curios and memorials associated with the principal events in American history. Conspicuous in the art collection is the wood-carved statue of Washington, by William Rush, and Benjamin West's painting of William Penn's Treaty with the Indians.

Congress Hall

THE Philadelphia County Building, now known as Congress Hall, had been part of the plan of the State House Row as laid out by Andrew Hamilton in 1732, and the ground had been bought four years later, but it was not until 1785 that the Assembly of Pennsylvania made an appropriation of $3,000 from the proceeds of the sale of the old "Philadelphia Gaol and Workhouse."

The building was completed and ready for use in 1789. The new government of the United States was just going into operation in New York, and the Assembly of Pennsylvania formally offered the use of the new County Building or any of the State House Row buildings in case Congress should make a choice of Philadelphia as temporary capital of the federal government. In Congress efforts were being made to establish the permanent seat of government in Virginia, Maryland, New Jersey, and Delaware, as well as Pennsylvania, and there was considerable debate. Finally a bill was passed deciding on a permanent capital on the banks of the Potomac, later to be known as the City of Wash-

Where Vice-Presidents John Adams and Thomas Jefferson presided. The Senate Chamber in Congress Hall, State House Row.

ington in the District of Columbia, the transfer of the government thence to be in 1800, and establishing temporary residence in Philadelphia. Accordingly, the third session of the First United States Congress met December 6, 1790, in the Philadelphia County Building, thereafter known as Congress Hall.

It was here that the essential features of the new government were adopted, the Constitution of the United States put in running order, the Army and Navy placed upon a creditable footing, the United States Mint established, and the States of Vermont, Kentucky, and Tennessee admitted to the Union.

And it was in Congress Hall that George Washington was inaugurated President, March 4, 1793, for his second term, and the second President, John Adams, inaugurated March 4, 1797,—Washington in the Senate Chamber and Adams in the House of Representatives. In the latter room Washington delivered his famous Farewell Address to the American people, in 1796.

The House of Representatives met on the lower floor of Congress, and the Senate Chamber was the large room on the second floor, the adjoining smaller rooms being used for committees. The Congress occupied the Congress Hall until the seat of government was removed to Washington in 1800.

The Supreme Court Building

PHILADELPHIA had built its first City Hall at Second and Market Streets, completing it in 1707. There, in the first Town House, or Guild Hall, as it was called, the Courts of the Province of Pennsylvania held

The House of Representatives in Congress Hall, Independence Square. A view from the visitors' gallery.

their sessions, including the Supreme Court established under Royal Charter to William Penn dated March 4, 1687. The County Courts,—Common Pleas, Orphans' Court, and Quarter Sessions,—also met in that building; the Corporation itself met and transacted business; the Mayor held his Court as Committing Magistrate; and there were a pillory and prison cage. When the State House was built, the offices and public records of the City were moved to the little east and west wings of that building, where they remained until after the Revolution.

In 1746 James Hamilton, then Mayor of Philadelphia, suggested to City Council that as it had been customary for the Mayor when leaving office to give an entertainment to the gentlemen of the Corporation of the City, he intended to offer in lieu thereof £150 to be laid out in something permanently useful to the City. He proposed that the money be applied toward "the erecting of an Exchange for the like uses with that of the Royal Exchange in London, or such other Publick Edifice as the Mayor and Comonalty shall see fit to order and direct." The proposal was approved, and this money, together with four similar gifts from succeeding mayors, was placed at interest by the City Treasurer.

It was decided, in 1775, to apply the money toward building a City Hall on the ground at Fifth and Chestnut Streets which had been placed in trust by the builder of the State House. But the Revolutionary War suspended all operations, although ten years later the Assembly appropriated £6000 from the sale of the old High Street Prison, and in 1789, $8,000 was raised by a

Old City Hall, at Fifth and Chestnut in State House Row, used as the United States Supreme Court Building between 1790 and 1800. To the rear is the building of the American Philosophical Society.

lottery. The next year the City Hall was begun, and within two years was completed. In outward appearance it closely resembles the Congress Hall on the other end of State House Row. It is of plain brick, two stories high, with a small cupola.

When the Federal Government came to Philadelphia, in 1790, the Federal Congress was granted the use of the County Building, while the State Assembly with the County Court were crowded into the State House. So the Federal Courts, Supreme, Circuit and District, as well as the State Supreme Court, were accommodated in this almost completed City Hall.

For ten years (1790-1800) the United States Supreme Court occupied the large room on the first floor of the City Hall. When the Court had first assembled in New York City in 1789 no cases were listed, so they had framed a simple code of rules and adjourned. But when they convened in Philadelphia cases were ready for them, and it was here that the first cases were tried. While this tribunal was passing through these formative years, it functioned with considerable smoothness, as did indeed the other branches of the new Government.

The Supreme Court had some intellectual men and it had brilliant men, and they well laid the national judicial foundation.

John Jay, of New York, was appointed Chief Justice by George Washington in 1789, and presided over its first sessions, being succeeded by Oliver Ellsworth, of Connecticut, from 1796 to 1800. The Associate Judges were John Rutledge, of South Carolina, William Cushing, of Massachusetts, James Wilson, of Pennsylvania,

Carpenter's Hall, where the First Continental Congress met. Continuously used since 1770 as the guild hall of the Carpenters' Company, which was instituted in 1724.

Samuel Chase, of Rhode Island, John Blair, of Virginia, James Iredell, of North Carolina, Thomas Johnson, of Maryland, William Paterson, of New Jersey, Bushrod Washington, of Virginia, and Alfred Moore, of North Carolina.

The United States Circuit and District Courts were held in the second story back room of the City Hall. After the seat of Federal Government was removed to Washington, the City Government again assumed charge of the building, and remained there until the consolidation of the City and Districts in 1854. "The Row" was used for courthouse purposes throughout a long period thereafter.

The First Continental Congress

WHILE it is true that Carpenters' Hall, where the First Continental Congress met, is in no way a part of State House Row, nevertheless the meeting of that Congress had a great deal to do with the events which followed and which gave State House Row its greatest fame.

The First Continental Congress met in Philadelphia on September 4, 1774, as a result of an agreement reached by the Committees of Correspondence in the various Colonies. The delegates included practically all the leading men of the Colonies, for the Congress was really an insurrectionary body with plenipotentiary powers. It was theoretically to remain in perpetual session, although the membership was constantly changing because of the necessity for delegates to return to important duties elsewhere.

The First Prayer in the Continental Congress, from a painting by T. H. Matteson. Rev. Jacob Duché, of Christ Church, leading in prayer in Carpenters' Hall.

When the First Continental Congress came to Philadelphia, the Provincial Assembly of Pennsylvania was in session at the State House. So the Carpenters' Company offered the use of their fine guild hall, at Fourth and Chestnut Streets, and it was accepted.

Peyton Randolph, of Virginia, was chosen President; and Charles Thomson, of Philadelphia, was appointed Secretary, a post which he held during the entire life of the Congress. There were two months' secret sessions, during which the disagreements with the King's government were thoroughly discussed; and the Congress adopted a Declaration of Rights, in which the political claims of the Colonies were clearly set forth, naming eleven different acts which they declared had been passed in violation of their rights since the accession of George III. They framed a memorial to the King and another to the people of England, making a last appeal before the resort to arms; and they formed an association to put a stop to all trade with Great Britain until the obnoxious laws should be repealed. The Congress provided for another meeting, to be held the following Spring, and then adjourned.

The membership of the First Continental Congress —

NEW HAMPSHIRE

John Sullivan	Nathaniel Folsom

MASSACHUSETTS

Thomas Cushing	Samuel Adams
John Adams	Robert Treat Paine

RHODE ISLAND

Stephen Hopkins	Samuel Ward

The First City Troop acting as a guard of honor to escort a notable visitor to Independence Square.

Connecticut

Eliphalet Dyer

Silas Deane

Roger Sherman

New York

Isaac Low

John Jay

William Floyd

Simon Boerum

John Haring

John Alsop

James Duane

Henry Wisner

Philip Livingston

New Jersey

James Kinsey

Stephen Crane

John De Hart

William Livingston

Richard Smith

Pennsylvania

Joseph Galloway

Charles Humphreys

Edward Biddle

George Ross

John Dickinson

Thomas Mifflin

John Morton

Samuel Rhoads

Delaware

Caesar Rodney

George Read

Thomas McKean

Maryland

Robert Goldsborough

Thomas Johnson

Samuel Chase

Matthew Tilghman

William Paca

Virginia

Peyton Randolph

George Washington

Richard Bland

Edmund Pendleton

Richard Henry Lee

Patrick Henry

Benjamin Harrison

The markets just off Dock Street. From a photographic study by John Allen.

North Carolina

William Hooper   Joseph Hewes
Richard Caswell

South Carolina

Henry Middleton   Thomas Lynch
Christopher Gadsen   John Rutledge
Edward Rutledge

The Governor of Georgia had succeeded in preventing any delegates from Georgia from attending the First Continental Congress.

The following is the roll of Presidents of the Continental Congress:—

Peyton Randolph, of Va.	Sept. 5, 1774
Henry Middleton, of S. C.	Oct. 22, 1774
Peyton Randolph	May 10, 1775
John Hancock, of Mass.	May 24, 1775
Henry Laurens, of S. C.	Nov. 1, 1777
John Jay, of N. Y.	Dec. 10, 1778
Samuel Huntington, of Conn.	Sept. 28, 1779
Thomas McKean, of Del.	July 10, 1781
John Hanson, of Md.	Nov. 5, 1781
Elias Boudinot, of N. J.	Nov. 4, 1782
Thomas Mifflin, of Pa.	Nov. 3, 1783
Richard Henry Lee, of Va.	Nov. 30, 1784
Nathaniel Gorman, of Mass.	June 6, 1786
Arthur St. Clair, of Pa.	Feb. 2, 1787
Cyrus Griffin, of Va.	Jan. 22, 1788

A tableau of the Adoption of the Declaration of Independence, posed in the actual Declaration Chamber, using the original furniture and, as in 1776, a few borrowed Windsor chairs.

The Declaration of Independence

THE Continental Congress re-assembled on May 10, 1775, in the State House in Philadelphia, now known as Independence Hall. The Congress met in the east room (since called the Declaration Chamber) and on July 4, 1776, enacted the Declaration of Independence. The circumstances of the adoption of that historic declaration are so often misunderstood that it would be well to quote from the Journal of the Congress. It should first be clearly held in mind that the number of delegates from the several States had no bearing on the passage of the Declaration of Independence, as each State had but one vote, although the States were authorized to send as many delegates to Congress as they wished.

June 7, 1776, resolution for Independence first introduced in Congress by Richard Henry Lee, of Virginia.

June 8, 1776, motion for Independence referred to "Committee of the Whole." John Hancock, President, yielded chair to Benjamin Harrison, of Virginia.

June 10, 1776, question debated during session by Committee. Adoption urged from floor by Richard Henry Lee, John Adams, George Wythe, Elbridge Gerry, Thomas McKean, Thomas Jefferson and Samuel Adams. Committee agreed to report to Congress the Resolution, adopted by vote of seven (7) Colonies to five (5). Question postponed till July 1, 1776.

June 11, 1776, Congress Resolved, That the

Resolved

that these United Colonies are, and of
right ought to be, free and independent States; that
they are absolved from all allegiance to the British
Crown, and that all political connection between them
and the state of Great Britain is, and ought to be,
totally dissolved.

A facsimile of the original autograph "Resolution respecting Independency," as submitted by Richard Henry Lee, June 7, 1776, voted July 2, by the Continental Congress, and incorporated in the Declaration of Independence as written by Thomas Jefferson.

Committee for preparing the Declaration consist of five. The members chosen being Thomas Jefferson, John Adams, Benjamin Franklin, Roger Sherman and Robert R. Livingston.

July 1, 1776, Congress resolved itself into Committee of the Whole to take into consideration the "Resolution respecting Independency," the Declaration itself being referred to the same body.

July 2, 1776, the Congress resumed the consideration of the resolution reported from the Committee of the Whole, which was agreed to as follows:

"RESOLVED, That these United Colonies are, and of right ought to be, Free and Independent States; that they are absolved from all allegiance to the British Crown, and that all political connection between them and the State of Great Britain is and ought to be totally dissolved."

July 3, 1776, Resolved, That the Congress will, tomorrow, again resolve itself into a Committee of the Whole to take into their further consideration the Declaration of Independence.

July 4, 1776, Congress resolved itself into a Committee of the Whole to take into further consideration the Declaration, and after some time the President resumed the chair and Mr. Harrison reported that the Committee had agreed to a Declaration which they desired him to report. The Declaration being read was agreed to.

The engrossed and signed Declaration of Independence, in the form in which
it has gone down into history.

Late on the afternoon of July 4, 1776, with John Hancock, of Massachusetts, as President of the Congress, and Charles Thomson, of Philadelphia, as Secretary, the Declaration of Independence was passed. The next day the Congress "*Resolved*, that copies of the Declaration be sent to the several Assemblies, Conventions, and Councils of Safety, and to the Several Commanding Officers of the Continental Troops, that it be proclaimed in each of the United States, and at the Head of the Army."

On July 8, 1776, the adoption by Congress of the Declaration was officially proclaimed, a ceremony which took place in the State House Yard at noon,—the first public proclamation of the document. It was read to the assembled townspeople by Colonel John Nixon, member of the Committee of Safety, who stood on the platform of the observatory which had been erected by the American Philosophical Society back of their building for the observation of the Transit of Venus, in 1769. There followed a great celebration. The welcome extended to the reading of the Declaration was enthusiastic in nearly every part of the country, the formal proclamation being made a holiday occasion at every point of public assemblage.

John Adams was of the opinion that "the second of July, 1776, will be the most memorable epoch in the history of America," that being the day of the adoption of Richard Henry Lee's resolution. But the Fourth of July was the day of the formal adoption of the Declaration, and beginning the very next year, the Glorious Fourth has always been enthusiastically celebrated as the birthday of the nation.

A Declaration by the Representatives of the UNITED STATES
OF AMERICA. in General Congress assembled

When in the course of human events it becomes necessary for a people to
dissolve the political bands which have connected them with another, and to
assume among the powers of the earth the separate and equal station to
which the laws of nature & of nature's god entitle them, a decent respect
to the opinions of mankind requires that they should declare the causes
which impel them to the separation.

We hold these truths to be self-evident; that all men are
created equal & independent; that from that equal creation they derive
rights inherent & inalienable, among which are the preservation of
life, & liberty, & the pursuit of happiness; that to secure these ends, go-

Facsimile of the rough draft of the first part of the Declaration of Independence, in the handwriting of Thomas Jefferson. Now in the possession of the government at Washington.

The actual writing of the Declaration of Independence was done by Thomas Jefferson, and the original draft was in his handwriting, with a few alterations by interlining in the handwriting of Benjamin Franklin and John Adams. The Congress ordered that the Declaration be fairly engrossed on parchment, but it was not until August that the work could be completed and on August 2, 1776, the historic document as engrossed was signed by the members of the Congress present, the remainder signing later. Some of the signers had not been members of the Congress on July 4, and some of the members of July 4 had been replaced before the date of the signing,—due to the need for their services elsewhere.

The following is a list of the names of the signers from the thirteen original States they represented:

Massachusetts Bay

John Adams	John Hancock
Samuel Adams	Robert Treat Paine
Elbridge Gerry	

Connecticut

Samuel Huntington	William Williams
Roger Sherman	Oliver Wolcott

New Jersey

Abraham Clark	Richard Stockton
Francis Hopkinson	John Witherspoon
John Hart	

Pennsylvania

George Clymer	Benjamin Rush
Benjamin Franklin	James Smith
John Morton	George Taylor
Robert Morris	James Wilson
George Ross	

The Declaration Chamber in Independence Hall, where the Declaration was adopted and the Constitution framed. On the dais are the original desk and "rising sun" chair and the inkwell.

DELAWARE

Thomas McKean　　　　　Caesar Rodney
George Read

MARYLAND

Charles Carroll of Carrollton　William Paca
Samuel Chase　　　　　Thomas Stone

RHODE ISLAND

William Ellery　　　　　Stephen Hopkins

NEW YORK

William Floyd　　　　　Francis Lewis
Philip Livingston　　　　Lewis Morris

VIRGINIA

Carter Braxton　　　　　Henry Richard Lee
Benjamin Harrison　　　　Thomas Nelson, Jr.
Thomas Jefferson　　　　George Wythe
Francis Lightfoot Lee

NORTH CAROLINA

Joseph Hewes　　　　　John Penn
William Hooper

SOUTH CAROLINA

Arthur Middleton　　　　Thomas Lynch, Jr.
Thomas Heyward　　　　Edward Rutledge

GEORGIA

Button Gwinnett　　　　George Walton
Lyman Hall

NEW HAMPSHIRE

Josiah Bartlett　　　　　William Whipple
Matthew Thornton

(335)

The PENNSYLVANIA EVENING POST.

Price only Two Coppers. Published every Tuesday, Thursday, and Saturday Evenings.

Vol. II.1 SATURDAY, JULY 6. 1776. [Num. 228.]

In CONGRESS, July 4, 1776.
A Declaration by the Representatives
of the United States of America,
in General Congress assembled.

WHEN, in the course of human events, it becomes necessary for one people to dissolve the
political bands which have connected them with
another, and to assume, among the powers of
the earth, the separate and equal station to which the laws of
nature and of nature's God intitle them, a decent respect to
the opinions of mankind requires that they should decl...
the causes which impel them to the separation....

We hold these truths to be self-evident, That ...
created equal; that they are endowed, by their ...
certain unalienable rights; that among the...
and the pursuit of happiness. That ...
governments are instituted amon...
power, from the consent of ...
form of government...
the right of the p...
true new gover...
ples, and...

He has dissolved Representative Houses repeatedly, for op-
posing with manly firmness his invasions on the rights of the
people.

He has refused for a long time, after such dissolution
cause others to be elected; whereby the legislati...
incapable of annihilation, have returned to
large for their exercise; the state remain...
exposed to all the dangers of invasion
vulsions within.

He has endeavour...
states, (...) that ...
tie...

...gs which ...
... And for the support
... reliance on the protection of
...m mutually pledge to each other ou...
...nes, and our sacred honor.

...ed by ORDER and in BEHALF of CONGRESS,
JOHN HANCOCK, President.
Attest. CHARLES THOMSON, Sec.

TO be SOLD, the brigantine TWO FRIENDS. She
is a prime sailor, but three years old, and carries
nine hundred and fifty, or a thousand barrels of flour.

The first publication of the Declaration in a newspaper, July 6, 1776.

The fifty-six signers of the Declaration of Independence represented a variety of vocations: twenty-four were lawyers, fourteen agriculturists, four physicians, one minister of the gospel and three former ministers, one manufacturer, and nine merchants. The longevity of the group has been remarked on. Three lived to be over 90 years of age, 10 over 80, 11 over 70, 14 over 60, 11 over 50, 6 over 44, and the other, at the age of 30, drowned at sea. The average age of the fifty-six men was over 62 years. By a singular coincidence, the deaths of John Adams and Thomas Jefferson occurred on the same day, July 4, 1826, the fiftieth anniversary of the adoption of the Declaration. Charles Carroll alone outlived these two.

Of all the historic collections made by assiduous hobbyists, few equal in eagerness of quest that with which complete collections of signatures of these fifty-six men are sought, and it is the irony of the situation that the most eagerly sought American signature, because the rarest in the market, is that of Button Gwinett, of Georgia, who had been perhaps the most obscure personage of the Congress, but certainly the signer of fewer other papers,—and therefore his is the most difficult signature to obtain.

The visitor to Independence Hall will observe that the east room is separated from the central hallway by a wall with a door, while the west room is separated only by open arches. The west room was so constructed because it was intended as a court room, with sessions open to the public; the east room was designed for the use of the Provincial Assembly, many of whose meetings

The southwestern corner in the State House Yard, or Independence Square, showing the Walnut Street gate with the Prison across the street. A Birch print, about 1799.

necessarily would be private. This explains why the Continental Congress held its sessions, and the Federal Constitutional Convention its sessions, in the east room.

The Articles of Confederation

ON THE same day that the Continental Congress appointed a committee to frame a Declaration of Independence, it appointed another to prepare Articles of Confederation. But it was not until November 15, 1777, that the Congress adopted the Articles of Confederation and Perpetual Union, providing for a single-chambered Congress with limited powers over war, peace, foreign affairs, coinage, and postal arrangements, able to raise money only by requisitions upon the States. In this Congress, each State had but one vote, and nine votes were necessary for important acts. The Articles of Confederation were signed July 9, 1778, by delegates of New Hampshire, Massachusetts, Rhode Island, Connecticut, New York, Pennsylvania, Virginia, and South Carolina. North Carolina signed July 21; Georgia, July 24; New Jersey, November 26; Delaware, May 5, 1779; Maryland, March 1, 1781. The following are the names of the signers:

NEW HAMPSHIRE

Josiah Bartlett   John Wentworth, Jr.

MASSACHUSETTS BAY

John Hancock   Francis Dana
Samuel Adams   James Lovell
Elbridge Gerry   Samuel Holten

The Penrose House on Washington Square, built about 1800. White marble stoop, eight-panel door, fanlight, railing, foot-scraper, twelve-pane window, Venetian blind, shutter, and brick pavement, are all characteristic of the period.

RHODE ISLAND AND PROVIDENCE PLANTATIONS
Wm. Ellery   John Collins
Henry Marchant
                    CONNECTICUT
Roger Sherman   Titus Hosmer
Samuel Huntington   Andrew Adams
Oliver Wolcott
                    NEW YORK
James Duane   William Duer
Francis Lewis   Gouverneur Morris
                    NEW JERSEY
John Witherspoon   Nathaniel Scudder
                    PENNSYLVANIA
Robert Morris   Wm. Clingan
Daniel Roberdeau   Joseph Reed
Jonathan Bayard Smith
                    DELAWARE
Thos. McKean   Nicholas Van Dyke
John Dickinson
                    MARYLAND
John Hanson   Daniel Carroll
                    VIRGINIA
Richard Henry Lee   John Harvie
John Banister   Francis Lightfoot Lee
Thomas Adams
                    NORTH CAROLINA
John Penn   John Williams
Cornelius Harnett
                    SOUTH CAROLINA
Henry Laurens   Richard Hutson
Wm. Henry Drayton   Thos. Heyward, Jr.
John Matthews
                    GEORGIA
John Walton   Edward Langworthy
Edward Telfair

--{ 133 }--

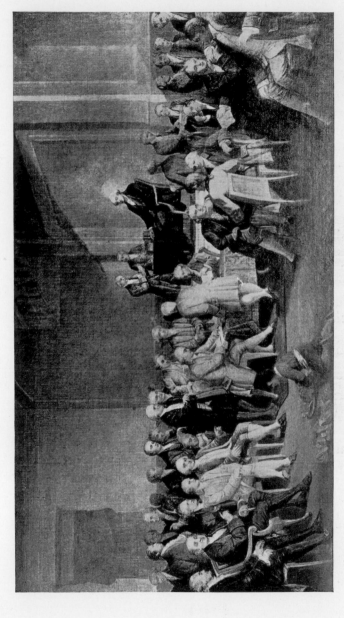

The Federal Constitutional Convention of 1787, from a study sketch in oil by David Rossiter, now in the Independence Hall collection.

The Federal Constitution

RATIFICATION of the Articles of Confederation by every State was necessary and was not secured until March 1, 1781. It speedily became evident that drastic alterations were necessary, whereupon the Annapolis Convention of 1786 called the Philadelphia Convention of 1787, which met in Independence Hall to formulate a Constitution to supersede the Articles of Confederation.

The Federal Convention conducted its sessions behind locked doors, with an injunction of secrecy on every member so strict and so respected that what was said and done at the meetings was not revealed until fifty years had passed, when James Madison, last of the survivors, died, and publication of his journal of the proceedings was permitted.

The first meeting was called to order on May 14, 1787, but the necessity for a quorum of seven States delayed matters for ten days, and some of the delegates did not arrive within another two months. Of the 73 delegates appointed, only 55 attended the Convention, and of these only 39 signed the Constitution at the end of their deliberations.

It should not be thought that the Constitution as it was finally framed was something that the thirteen States were eagerly awaiting, for they were by no means agreed on the principle of a strong central government. In fact, several of the States sent delegates expressly charged to combat such a plan, and several highly influential leaders declined to act as delegates because

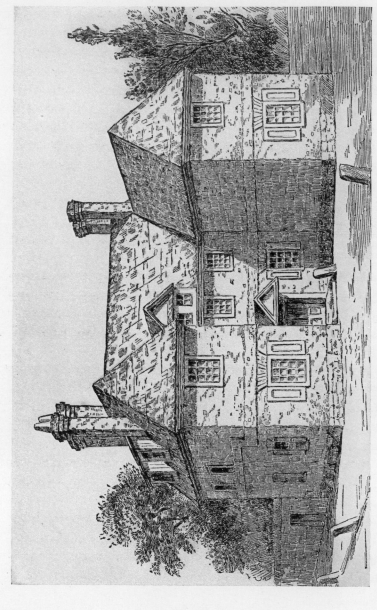

The Slate Roof House, Philadelphia home of William Penn, and the Provincial seat of government under both Penn and Logan. From an old print.

of the same prejudice. Nor was that strange, for the various colonies had been founded and developed upon radically different religions, interests, and conditions. The New Englanders, for example, seemed almost like a different race from the Virginians, and the New Yorkers from the Carolinians, and so on. The remarkable thing was there were leaders of sufficient capacity to be able to fight through to success their determination, based on a large-minded foresightedness, that the thirteen groups should be welded into one great group,—that in union there is strength just as clearly in peace as in war.

The new Constitution presented a new conception, of a government of the people of the United States,—"a synthesis, and not a mere assembly," a federal and not a confederate government. It was not without significance that the engrossed copy of the document, as signed, began, in great lettering: "WE THE PEOPLE" and not "We the States."

It had been agreed in advance of the formal opening that George Washington should preside. He was nominated by Pennsylvania and unanimously elected. The man who had led the Continental Armies in winning that Independence so eloquently declared by Congress in this very room eleven years before, presided as President of this Convention. Major William Jackson was elected Secretary.

The members of the Convention did not realize how completely reconstructive their work was to be. Most of them were uncertain as to whether they were going to patch up the Articles of Confederation or blaze a new trail.

Sixth Street, south from Walnut Street along Washington Square, as it looked between 1837 and 1913. A row of fashionable homes which, like those on Walnut Street from Sixth to Seventh, became lawyers' offices.

The main division of opinion in the Convention was as to whether in the new Government one State's influence should be equal to that of any other State or should be based on population. Edmund Randolph, of Virginia, submitted a plan favoring representation according to population in both Houses, while William Paterson, of New Jersey, submitted a plan proposing an equal vote for each State and only one house. William Samuel Johnson, of Connecticut, proposed a compromise: two houses, a Senate, with equal representation and a House of Representatives with proportionate representation. After considerable debate this compromise was effected and it was adopted.

The second division of opinion was with regard to Governmental regulation of commerce. Both export and import taxes were proposed. Charles Cotesworth Pinckney declared that South Carolina could not enter the Union if exports were to be taxed, for practically her whole wealth lay in the export of rice. So export duties were rejected, but Federal control over commerce was conceded.

Georgia, North Carolina, and South Carolina refused to enter the Union if the slave traffic was to be prohibited; so the third compromise was to the agreement that Congress should not prohibit the slave trade until later and that a fugitive slave law should be provided.

The Constitution thus completed, after four hot summer months of careful work, was then submitted to the Continental Congress, who discussed it for eight days and then voted that it be "transmitted to the several State legislatures in order to be submitted to a

The Walnut Street Theatre, at Ninth and Walnut Streets, the oldest playhouse in the country. Edwin Forrest made his debut and since 1809 most of the distinguished actors and actresses have appeared here.

convention of delegates in each State by the people thereof in conformity to the resolves of the Convention."

The thirteen States ratified the Constitution in the order following:

Delaware, December 6, 1787; Pennsylvania, December 12, 1787; New Jersey, December 18, 1787; Georgia, January 2, 1788; Connecticut, January 9, 1788; Massachusetts, February 6, 1788; Maryland, April 28, 1788; South Carolina, May 23, 1788; New Hampshire, June 21, 1788; Virginia, June 25, 1788; New York, June 26, 1788; North Carolina, November 21, 1789; Rhode Island, May 29, 1790.

The names of the Signers of the Constitution follow, together with the names of those who for various reasons were absent when the Constitution was signed or who refused to sign, given in *italics*:

NEW HAMPSHIRE

John Langdon   Nicholas Gilman

MASSACHUSETTS

Elbridge Gerry   Rufus King
Nathaniel Gorham   *Caleb Strong*

CONNECTICUT

William Samuel Johnson   *Oliver Ellsworth*
Roger Sherman

NEW YORK

Robert Yates   *John Lansing*
Alexander Hamilton

NEW JERSEY

William Livingston   William Patterson
David Brearley   Jonathan Dayton
William Churchill Houston

Dr Sir

May 26. 1798

Your Not of to day I have receivd. your letter to the Conveying Van shall be conformed & realized

Be assurd I think properly of your efforts to save the Pennsylvania Property Company.   A matter has turnd up to day which make it very desirable that I should see you in the Morning, come here therefore at Nine or in Black in the Morning I will not keep you half an hour   You body knows of my asking you to come I course no injure

Yours sincerely
RobtMorris

Jn° Nicholson Esq

A letter written by Robert Morris to John Nicholson while Morris was confined in the debtors' apartment of the Walnut Street Prison.   The original letter is now in the possession of the Penn Mutual Life Insurance Company, whose office is on the site of the prison.

PENNSYLVANIA

Benjamin Franklin
Thomas Mifflin
Robert Morris
George Clymer

Thomas Fitzsimmons
Jared Ingersoll
James Wilson
Gouverneur Morris

DELAWARE

George Read
Gunning Bedford, Jr.
John Dickinson

Richard Bassett
Jacob Broom

MARYLAND

James McHenry
Daniel of St. Thomas
Jenifer

Daniel Carroll
John Francis Mercer
Luther Martin

VIRGINIA

George Washington
Edmund Randolph
John Blair
James Madison

George Mason
George Wythe
James McClurg

NORTH CAROLINA

Alexander Martin
William Richardson Davie
William Blount

Richard Dobbs Spaight
Hugh Williamson

SOUTH CAROLINA

John Rutledge
Charles Cotesworth
Pinckney

Charles Pinckney
Pierce Butler

GEORGIA

William Few
Abraham Baldwin

William Pierce
William Houston

The Morris House, at 225 South Eighth Street, built in 1786. A beautiful survivor of a graceful day in architecture.

Of those who signed their names to the Federal Constitution, the six following were signers of the Declaration of Independence:

Roger Sherman　　　　George Clymer
Benjamin Franklin　　James Wilson
Robert Morris　　　　George Read

and the five following were signers of the Articles of Confederation:

Roger Sherman　　　　John Dickinson
Robert Morris　　　　Daniel Carroll
Gouverneur Morris

The Liberty Bell

CONVINCED that nowhere in the American provinces could be produced a bell of sufficient proportions, the superintendents of the State House wrote to the Colonial agent of the Province in London, November 1, 1751, as follows:

"Respected Friend, Robert Charles,—The Assembly having ordered us (the Superintendents of the State House) to procure a bell from England, to be purchased for their use, we take the liberty to supply ourselves to thee to get us a good bell, of about two thousand pounds weight, the cost of which, we presume may amount to about one hundred pounds sterling, or, perhaps, with the charges, something more, and accordingly we have enclosed a first bill of exchange. . . .

"We hope and rely on thy care and assistance in this affair, and that thou wilt procure and forward it by the first good opportunity, as our workmen inform

The Liberty Bell as it now appears in the tower hallway of Independence Hall.

us it will be much less trouble to hang the bell before their scaffolds are struck from the building where we intend to place it, which will not be done till the end of next summer or beginning of the fall. Let the bell be cast by the best workmen, and examined carefully before it is shipped, with the following words well shaped in large letters round it, *viz:*—

"*By order of the Assembly of the Province of Pennsylvania, for the State House in the City of Philadelphia, 1752.*

"And underneath,

"*Proclaim Liberty through all the land to all the inhabitants thereof.—Levit. xxv. 10.*

"As we have experienced thy readiness to serve this Province on all occasions, we desire it may be our excuse for this additional trouble from thy assured friends.

Isaac Norris.

Thomas Leech.

Edward Warner.

"Let the package for transportation be examined with particular care, and the full value insured there."

The bell duly arrived, ten months later, but "upon its being hung up [on trusses, in the State House Yard] to try the sound, it was cracked by a stroke of the clapper without any other violence." While the superintendents were endeavoring to have it returned to England, "two ingenious workmen undertook to cast it here. . . . When we broke up the metal, our judges generally agreed it was too high and brittle,

The first journey of the Liberty Bell, a painting by E. W. Deming, in the Wanamaker & Brown store. Guarded by two hundred North Carolina and Virginia cavalrymen, the Liberty Bell was conveyed in the heavy baggage train of the Army, away from Philadelphia, which the British (September of 1777) were about to occupy, and so taken to Allentown for safety, where it was hidden in Zion Reformed Church.

and cast several little bells out of it to try the sound and strength, and fixed upon a mixture of an ounce and a half of copper to one pound of the old bell, and in this proportion we now have it.''

The "two ingenious workmen" of the above letter were Pass, a Maltese, and Stow, a Philadelphian. Although they had "made the mould in a masterly manner, and run the metal well," this second bell, after being hung up in its place, was found to contain too much copper, and Pass and Stow "were so tiezed with the witticisms of the town" that they asked and received permission to cast it once again. In June of 1753 the third casting, which is the bell of history, was finally hung in the steeple.

The inscription as it was finally cast on the Liberty Bell is not precisely as was ordered of the English founder. The Scriptural verse was placed above, instead of below, the other line; there are slight changes in wording; and of course the names of the founders and the place and year of recasting were substituted for the English bell-maker's mark. The inscription actually reads as follows:

PROCLAIM LIBERTY THROUGHOUT ALL THE LAND UNTO ALL THE INHABITANTS THEREOF.—LEV. xxv. 10.

BY ORDER OF THE ASSEMBLY OF THE PROVINCE OF PENSYLVANIA FOR THE STATE HOUSE IN PHILADA.
PASS AND STOW
PHILADA.
MDCCLIII

Independence Hall, the State House of Pennsylvania, as it looked in 1778—the Charles Willson Peale engraving, showing the "grandfather's clock" and the sheds for housing visiting Indians.

The word *Pennsylvania* lacks an *n* and a curious monogram of *v* and *s* is used for *verse*, before *10*.

The State House clock of the Revolutionary War period dated about the same time. It was not in the tower, but in the main building, with a clockface at either end, under the peaked roof, and with a white stone case running on down to the pavement, giving the effect of an enormous grandfather's clock at each end of the building. The man who took charge of this clock during the fateful year of 1776 was David Rittenhouse, the astronomer.

The Liberty Bell was intended to be rung on public occasions, such as the times of meeting of the Assembly and of courts of justice, but it was so frequently used for other than governmental purposes,—for fire and church calls, especially, that "divers inhabitants living nearby" made complaint by petition. The Liberty Bell was performing its function when on July 8, 1776, it rang to call a meeting of the citizens in State House Yard to hear the reading of the Declaration of Independence, and, ringing, led the celebration.

In 1828 a new clock was ordered for Independence Hall, to be placed in the tower, and a new bell to strike the hours with a hammer operated by the clockworks. The old Liberty Bell (in 1781 brought down behind the rose windows in the brick tower) was thereafter rung only upon special occasions. In the Centennial year another new clock and another new bell were installed, the gift of a public-spirited citizen. A singular fatality seems to have attended these State House bells, for the bell of 1828, and the bell of 1876, like the original bell of 1753, each had to be recast.

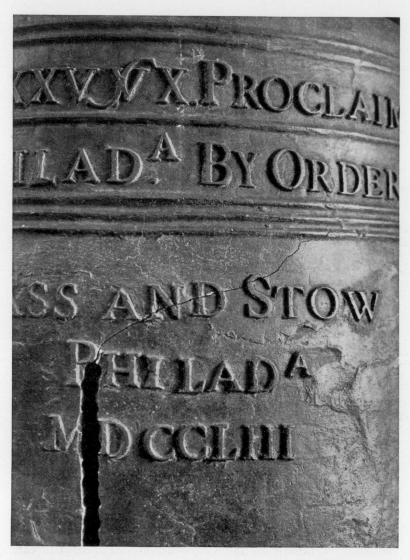

A detail of the Liberty Bell, showing how the crack was tooled out in an attempt to prevent its extension, also showing the "verse" monogram.

The Liberty Bell was cracked July 8, 1835,—exactly fifty-nine years after the day it had fulfilled its prophetic inscription,—while tolling for the death of Chief Justice Marshall. It had lived out eighty-two years of usefulness; it had called the people together to preserve their rights under the British crown; it had recorded many important events of the Revolution and of the early days of the nation; it had celebrated the proclamation of the Declaration of Independence.

Some years later the crack was bored out in an unsuccessful attempt to prevent further cracking and perhaps even restore the tone. This explains why the crack, at the present time, is so remarkably large. If you will examine closely, you will see that above the great crack a hairline crack extends some distance beyond. It is to prevent a complete splitting that a "spider" framework has been placed inside the Bell, holding it rigid.

The first time the Liberty Bell was removed from Philadelphia was on September 18, 1777; the British Army being about to occupy the city, the Bell was taken down and conveyed to Allentown, Pa., where it was hidden for almost a year in Zion Reformed Church, so that it might not be captured and melted into cannon. A trolley line known as "The Liberty Bell Route" long followed the actual route taken by the Bell from Chestnut Hill to Allentown. Since that occasion the Bell has made journeys to New Orleans, Chicago, Atlanta, Charleston, S. C., Boston, St. Louis, and San Francisco. In each case the journey was the occasion for a continuous round of celebration by patriots

The cobble-stone driveway from Sixth Street into Independence Square.

coming from long distances with the hope of catching a glimpse of the venerated relic, and perhaps even touching it.

If, as you walk through Independence Square, you will look up at the tower of Independence Hall, you can see the present day bell in the belfry. The inscription on this successor of the Liberty Bell repeats the original prophecy:

> PROCLAIM LIBERTY THROUGHOUT
> ALL THE LAND UNTO ALL THE
> INHABITANTS THEREOF.

and adds another Scriptural verse:

> GLORY TO GOD IN THE HIGHEST,
> AND ON EARTH PEACE, GOOD
> WILL TOWARD MEN.